THE IDEAL
REALIZED

THE IDEAL REALIZED

Practical Instructions from Neville Goddard

EDITED AND INTRODUCED
BY MITCH HOROWITZ

MEDIA

Published 2020 by Gildan Media LLC
aka G&D Media
www.GandDmedia.com

First Edition: 2020

Front cover design by David Rheinhardt of Pyrographx

Interior design by Meghan Day Healey of Story Horse, LLC.

Library of Congress Cataloging-in-Publication Data is available upon request

ISBN: 978-1-7225-0165-5

10   9   8   7   6   5   4   3   2   1

CONTENTS

Contents

The Triumph of Imagination

By Mitch Horowitz

"The inner journey must never be without direction."
—Neville, *Awakened Imagination*, 1954

It is my hope that you will find this a wholly original kind of anthology of Neville Goddard's works. Although collections of Neville's lectures and books abound, this one is designed with a special purpose. *The Ideal Realized* distills specific passages from Neville's work that are focused on concrete methods. The aim of this book is to provide you with a reference source for the full range of techniques that the teacher offered across his career, and thus help you to exercise the powers of your mind more fully and quickly.

In that vein, I have curated references from early in Neville's literary career in 1939 to just before the teacher's death in 1972. One of his final lectures that year, "Even the Wicked," concludes the anthology portion of this book. I provide dates and, where possible, locales of his talks. In some cases, I abridge or excerpt passages from longer works in order to focus on a specific technique. Abridged passages are indicated by ellipses (. . .). The bibliographical material allows you to locate the fuller source if you wish. I also italicize key lines and paragraphs to highlight specific applications.

My afterword, "Chariot of Fire," reproduces for the first time my earliest talk on Neville in June 2013. It offers further ideas about optimizing his methods, highlights some of my personal efforts, and provides the broader historical background of Neville's ideas and techniques. I think you will find it a useful companion to the writings in this volume. The book is finally rounded out with a timeline of Neville's life and a selection of his aphorisms.

Occult philosopher Israel Regardie (1907–1985) encountered Neville in New York City in 1946 and wrote glowingly about him in his book *The Romance of Metaphysics*. Regardie greatly admired Neville but, for the all of the promise he saw in Neville's methods and for all the gravity he detected in Neville as an individual, Regardie also believed that Neville, at least at that stage of his career, had done too little to provide his audience with training and technique. The writer believed that Neville's injunction to enter the "feeling state" of your wish fulfilled—the lever of his system—was offered with too little practical instruction, at least for the everyday person. Regardie felt that Neville, as a former actor, dancer, and stage performer, might find it easier than most people to enter and remain in an emotive state. It is worth considering Regardie's perspective in full:

> Whether the average person can do this is another matter. Certainly some people can do it. Neville, I am sure, can do it. But he is an artist, a dancer. He has been enabled by his training, by his life's discipline, to assume a definite role. He can adopt a certain part, acting it out as though it were true. His is the ability and capacity to achieve identification with mental images, with a personality other than his own—that is an intrinsic part of his emotional make-up. That is why such states of consciousness are open and available to him—as naturally they are to similarly trained and similarly constituted people.
>
> But John Doe is not, I am afraid, capable of such unrestrained flights of feeling and imagination. His mind has become entirely too prosaic,

his feelings too inhibited, his imagination entirely too restrained for such flights into the empyrean. I do not say that in the last analysis that such feats are impossible to the average person. But I do insist that training is necessary—training in the art of "letting go," in the discipline of feeling, and in the analysis of psychological states. This takes such time and effort that there are few willing to embark upon a way of life that implies the expenditure of much time and labor. But if they do not wish to do so, then such states of consciousness and such spiritual achievements must remain mere dreams, fantasies, visions of another world completely beyond their reach.

Though my sympathies are largely with Neville both as to many of his conceptions and technical procedures—yet I feel that several factors are absent from his method. He is absolutely correct in placing emphasis on "feeling." By means of this intensity of feeling, all things become possible.

But the problem is to provoke such an intensity, a storm, a madness of emotion by means of which a communion with the unconscious self may be established. This certainly has not been adequately dealt with. Moreover, Neville advises relaxation. One must relax to the point of "floating," and losing awareness of one's body. But how shall we achieve such deep relaxation? This is not easy for most of us. What instruction does Neville give?

"You take your attention away from your problem and place it upon your being. You say silently but feelingly, 'I AM.' Simply feel that you are faceless and formless and continue doing so until you feel yourself floating.

"'Floating' is a psychological state which completely denies the physical. Through practice, in relaxation and willingly refusing to react to sensory impressions, it is found to develop a state of consciousness of pure receptivity."

I feel inclined to wager large odds that most who hear him or any other teacher of metaphysics, have not the least notion as to how to relax. There is nothing metaphysical in relaxation. By following a few simple rules which operate in accordance with known physiological and psychological laws, a deep state of freedom from neuro-muscular tension can be induced . . .

Moreover and far more important—what shall we do about developing this intensity of feeling? Merely to relax will not do it. One can relax, lose complete consciousness of the body, "float" beautifully away from awareness of sense and mind—and still be as cold-blooded as a fish. Neville's method is sound enough. But the difficulty is that few people are able to muster up this emotional exaltation or this intellectual concentration which are the royal approaches to the citadel of the Unconscious. As a result of this definite lack of training or technique, the mind wanders all over the place, and a thousand and one things totally unrelated to "I AM" are ever before their attention.

I believe that the ancients had superior methods. Confronted by the same problems, and by the same lack of training, they evolved methods which have stood the test of time. To some people they prescribed a long course of psychological training, having as its logical objective the development of a tremendous power of mental concentration. This training we have come to know as Yoga. To others not temperamentally capable of this, or unwilling to engage upon such a discipline, arduous to the extreme, they worked out other methods.

Anything that will tend to exalt the mind and feelings, is useful. Music, color, poetry, perfumes— anything that will intoxicate the mind and senses within certain limits, is utilisable . . .

When I wrote my first article about Neville in early 2005, I quoted Regardie's critique to a colleague.

He waved it off saying that the occult philosopher "didn't get it." I urge no side-stepping of Regardie's criticism. His wording and emphases are not my own, but he raises important points, asking whether the everyday person is capable of the relaxation required to enter a sustained *feeling state*, which is the royal road to mental causation in Neville's method. Perhaps things have grown easier in this regard since Regardie's era, as many of us are now schooled in meditative and mindfulness techniques. But I am still haunted by his points.

The Ideal Realized focuses on methods, most of them from Neville's own teachings, to aid in that relaxation. Many of these methods involve visualizing while in a near-sleep state, which sleep researchers today call *hypnagogia*. You experience this state naturally twice a day: just as you are drifting off at night and again as you are waking in the morning. During this stage between sleep and wakefulness, you experience dreamlike imagery and yet retain conscious awareness. It is a uniquely supple and suggestible frame of mind. Serious psychical researchers have found that hypnagogia is a heightened period for statistically recorded episodes of ESP phenomena. (I write further about this in *The Miracle Club* and *One Simple Idea*.) Neville had an early instinct for the uses of hypnagogia.

*   *   *

In another pillar of Neville's system—one that raises further questions of technique—change is said to occur not only from your assumptions about yourself but also about others. In his 1945 work *Prayer: The Art of Believing* (which is reproduced in full this collection), Neville writes: "To change the world, you must first change your conception of it. To change a man, you must change your conception of him. You must believe him to be the man you want him to be and mentally talk to him as though he were."

But what if you encounter a situation where, try as you might, you *cannot change your conception of another person, perhaps someone who torments you*? Sometimes people wrestle with forgiveness and re-conceptions of another person for years without results. I do not blame anyone for this, as unfinished emotional business can trenchantly linger, and sometimes for sound reasons. If you find yourself in such a predicament, are the doors of mental reconstruction closed to you? I believe they are not. To say that the doors of mental causation are closed would only serve to replicate the binary qualities of sin and salvation that many people who follow Neville's way of thought fled from in the religions of their childhood.

Rather, I believe that you should trust your own intellect and maturity by entering into an ameliorative mental state that you believe reflects *the highest current resolution of the situation for you*. Perhaps you cannot enter into a feeling state of beneficence toward a tormentor. But you may be able to enter into a feeling state of distance. Or, frankly, of self-defense. There may be instances where that is called for. Moreover, perhaps it is all that you can summon at a given point. Allow this. You must adopt a state that is *emotionally persuasive* to you, even if it is incremental. Use the tools that you have—do not feel bound by the imperative to view another in just one way.

Some people who love Neville's work may find this heterodox. It is not. Neville himself states in the lecture "Law of Assumption" in this volume: "Each man must find the means best suited to his nature to control his attention and concentrate it on the desired state." To this I would add, concentrate on the *best possible* desired state.

On a related note, I am frequently asked about how to structure affirmations. My response is always: there is no wrong way. Again, the vital element is *emotional persuasiveness*. We enact what we believe. Even if you feel compelled to frame your affirmation in future-tense, for example, or to condition it in some other way, I advise not struggling with that.

Your life and search are your own—and myriad responses, sometimes based on different needs, contingencies, or intervals of time, are wholly necessary. I believe that self-trust is an inherent part of mental causation. Respond to your needs. Frame your needs in ways that feel most natural for now. If your course must be indirect, allow that. If your course later alters, allow that too.

You may also find that an "indirect" path leads exactly where you need to go.

Another method by which to enter the desired state of mental creativity is the construction or re-construction of the *inner story* that you frame around yourself. The manner in which you view yourself—your ideals, your values, your persona, your purpose—is a vital source of power. As I was approaching this topic, I received a mysteriously well-timed letter from a reader in Utah. He framed exactly what I was after. With my correspondent's permission, his letter and my reply appear below:

Dear Mitch,

First of all, thank you so much for the work you're doing. I came across Neville when I was about 20 years old and his work shattered my reality in the best way possible. It's amazing to see someone like yourself that is dedicating his life to sharing his ideas, among others, with the world.

Second, I have a question that I would appreciate your input on. I'll try to make it as brief as possible.

When most hear the phrase, "Your thoughts create your reality" I feel like most are immediately directed to the everyday "chatter" that is going on between their ears. From there, they spend their time trying to forcefully stop the flow of thoughts. That's how it was for me. However, I'm beginning to understand that statement from a much deeper perspective and would love your opinion on it.

Is it not so much that the chatter creates our reality but more so the story we tell ourselves that creates our reality? Our story being our interpretation, true or false, regarding circumstances and our relationship to them.

For instance, a child may grow up thinking that they are ugly because one day in 6th grade, they decided to wear a new haircut. Later that day, they got bullied. They make the assumption that they're ugly and that's why they were bullied. When in reality, the bully is getting abused at home and is just simply taking it out on the kid. It could have been anyone.

Whether real or not, the victim interpreted it as such and has grown up thinking they are ugly. Now they are 46 years old and still think they're ugly and that expresses itself through failing relationships, lack of confidence, etc.

Not really sure how to connect the dots here and turn it into a practical means of creating a new and better reality. I guess that's what I'm hoping you can assist me with.

Appreciate any response to this.

Thank you Mitch.

Truman Mylin
Salt Lake City, UT

Hello Truman,

Your observation is remarkably well timed as I am writing about this issue right now.

It occurs to me that so much depends on what story we find emotionally persuasive about ourselves. How do you see yourself archetypally? That informs what to strive for as well as your belief in your ability to attain it. For example, as I just wrote someone, if you leave corporate America you may lose your health insurance. But maybe that's okay? These are the kinds of issues one can address more broadly in devising a new self-picture. We are so persuaded of what we can and cannot do, what we can and cannot attain, that we sometimes resist mental images of a richer, fuller life, however defined.

I believe it is possible to bypass conditioned resistance by reframing your sense of story. To pick up on your example, we see this occur all the time in the lives of people who may actually look rather ordinary in certain settings or clothing but who take on truly extraordinary new dimensions when they reconceive of themselves through fashion (a field I believe that the spiritual culture does not fully appreciate), adoption of new physical traits and tones, bodily adornment, and so forth. It is the outer telling of a new self-story. It is profoundly effective.

Personally speaking, I identify with rebels, from Henry David Thoreau to Joe Strummer. That identification can make it difficult for me to think in terms of accumulating money. Intellectually I want money—it has natural uses and fills vital needs—but I suspect that something in my self-story is in conflict with it. What if I can reframe that story so that I do not throw away the archetypes of rebellion but I somehow revise them to better encompass money? Norman Mailer was a rebel who wrote bestselling books. Steve Jobs was a rebel who upended digital culture. These are offhanded examples of how a revised self-story can help us enter the feeling state that is the royal road to mental causation.

I hope this is useful.

Thanks and best,

-Mitch-

If you want to gain a better understanding of Neville ideas about feeling states and effortlessness, I advise making a parallel reading of the work of someone whom Neville never directly mentions but whose ideas and phrasing appear in in his early work: French mind theorist Emile Coué (1857–1926).

Coué is famous for the mantra: "Day by day, in every way, I am getting better and better." But the mind theorist's career covered more than that. Coué was one of the earliest figures in modern life who understood the psychological impact of self-image, assumption, and imagination. A better summation of Coué's career than his famous mantra might be: *Imagination is destiny.*

An idea of Coué's that figured into Neville's thought—you can find this language in *Prayer: The Art of Believing*—is that each of us contains two competing forces: *will* and *imagination.* The will is your self-determinative and decision-making ability. Imagination consists of the mental pictures, conditioned responses, and assumptions that govern you, particularly with regard to self-image and emo-tional judgments about others. Coué said that when *will* and *imagination* clash, imagination invariably wins. Assumptions and conditioning almost always overcome intellect. As Neville put it in *Prayer*: "When belief and will are in conflict, belief invari-ably wins."

In a 1953 lecture reprinted in this collection as "Prayer Is a Surrender," Neville describes the need for an exquisitely gentle redirecting of your psy-che: "The sovereign rule is to make no effort, and if this is observed, you will intuitively fall into the right attitude." This echoes Coué from his 1922 book *Self-Mastery Through Conscious Autosuggestion*: "The sovereign rule is to make no effort, and if this is observed, you will intuitively fall into the right attitude."

There are many divergences in the two men's ideas, but from a parallel reading of Coué—whose work offers vibrant insights of its own—you will begin to glean a fuller idea of the importance of *effortless effort*. In short, Coué believed that you could recondition yourself from within a mild hyp-notic state (he was trained as hypnotist); Coué wrote that this is actually what is occurring when you use mantras or affirmations during hypnago-gia. Neville, too, discusses hypnosis in *Prayer*. (For a further exploration of Coué, you can read my article,

"The Man Who Helped the Beatles Admit It's Getting Better: The techniques of forgotten mind pioneer Émile Coué are simple, but they work," 2019, *Medium*.)

In this collection you will also find Neville's passages on dream interpretation, analysis of numbers and symbols, the use of objects for meditation, and the uses and misuses of speech. Each of these passages will help you in your journey to apply his ideas.

The genius of Neville's work is ultimately—and, I think it's fair to argue, exclusively—in its practicality. This volume is intended as a blueprint toward that end. My every wish is that you discover your own pathways and achievements within these pages, and that you share what you find.

CHAPTER 1

"Man Has Placed too Little Value on Himself"

From *At Your Command*, 1939

... Man's world in its every detail is his consciousness out-pictured. *You can no more change your environment, or world, by destroying things than you can your reflection by destroying the mirror.* Your environment, and all within it, reflects that which you are in consciousness. As long as you continue to be that in consciousness so long will you continue to out-picture it in your world.

Knowing this, begin to revalue yourself. Man has placed too little value upon himself. In the *Book of Numbers* you will read, "In that day there were giants in the land; and we were in our own sight as grasshoppers. And we were in their sight as grasshoppers." This does not mean a time in the dim past when man had the stature of giants. Today is the day—the eternal now—when conditions round about you have attained the appearance of giants (such as unemployed, the armies of your enemy, your problems and all things that seem to threaten you) those are the giant that make you feel yourself to be a grasshopper. But, you are told, you were first, in your own sight a grasshopper and because of this you were to the giants—a grasshopper. In other words, *you can only be to others what you are first to yourself.* Therefore, to revalue yourself and begin to feel yourself to be the giant, a center of power, is to dwarf these former giants and make of them grasshoppers . . .

. . . This being true, why not become aware of being great; God-loving; wealthy; healthy; and all attributes that you admire?

It is just as easy to possess the consciousness of these qualities as it is to possess their opposites for you have not your present consciousness because of your world. On the contrary, your world is what it is because of your present consciousness. Simple, is it not? Too simple in fact for the wisdom of man that tries to complicate everything . . .

. . . Before man can attempt to transform his world he must first lay the foundation—"I AM the Lord." That is, man's awareness, his consciousness of being is God. Until this is firmly established so that no suggestion or argument put forward by others can shake it, he will find himself returning to the slavery of his former beliefs. "If ye believe not that I AM he, ye shall die in your sins." That is, you shall continue to be confused and thwarted until you find the cause of your confusion. When you have lifted up the son of man then shall you know that I AM he, that is, that I, John Smith, do nothing of myself, but my father, or that state of consciousness which I am now one with does the works . . .

. . . A proof of this established consciousness is given you in the words, "Thank you, father." *When you come into the joy of thanksgiving so that you actually feel grateful for having received that which is not yet apparent to the senses, you have definitely become one in consciousness with the thing for which you gave thanks.* God (your awareness) is not mocked. You are ever receiving that which you are aware of being and no man gives thanks for something which he has not received. "Thank you father" is not, as it is used by many today a sort of magical formula. *You need never utter aloud the words, "Thank you, father."* In applying this principle as you rise in consciousness to the point where you are really grateful and happy for having received the thing desired, you automatically rejoice and give thanks inwardly. You have already accepted the gift which was but a desire before you rose in consciousness, and your faith is now the substance that shall clothe your desire . . .

. . . His name is not a name that you pronounce with the lips. You can ask forever in the name of God or Jehovah or Christ Jesus and you will ask in vain. 'Name' means nature; so, when you ask in the nature of a thing, results ever follow. *To ask in the name is to rise I consciousness and become one in nature with the thing desired, rise in consciousness to the nature of the thing, and you will become that thing in expression.*

Therefore, "what things soever ye desire, when ye pray, believe that ye receive them and ye shall receive them."

Praying, as we have shown you before, is recognition—the injunction to believe that ye receive is first person, present tense. This means that you must be in the nature of the things asked for before you can receive them.

To get into the nature easily, general amnesty is necessary. We are told, "Forgive if ye have aught against any, that your father also, which is in Heaven, may forgive you. But if ye forgive not, neither will your father forgive you."

This may seem to be some personal God who is pleased or displeased with your actions but this is not the case.

Consciousness, being God, if you hold in consciousness anything against man, you are binding that condition in your world. But to release man from all condemnation is to free yourself so that you may rise to any level necessary; there is therefore, no condemnation to those in Christ Jesus.

Therefore, a very good practice before you enter into your meditation is first to free every man in the world from blame. For law is never violated and you can rest confidently in the knowledge that every man's conception of himself is going to be his reward. So you do not have to bother yourself about seeing whether or not man gets what you consider he should get. For life makes no mistakes and always gives man that which man first gives himself.

This brings us to that much abused statement of the Bible on tithing. *Teachers of all kinds have enslaved man with this affair of tithing, for not themselves understanding the nature of tithing and being themselves fearful of lack, they have led their followers to believe that a tenth part of their income should be given to the Lord.* Meaning, as they make very clear, that, when one gives a tenth part of his income to their particular organization he is giving his "tenth part" to the Lord—(or is tithing). But remember, "I AM" the Lord." Your awareness of being is the God that you give to and you ever give in this manner.

Therefore when you claim yourself to be any-thing, you have given that claim or quality to God. And your awareness of being, which is no respecter of persons, will return to you pressed down, shaken together, and running over with that quality or attribute which you claim for yourself.

Awareness of being is nothing that you could ever name. To claim God to be rich; to be great; to be love; to be all wise; is to define that which cannot be defined. For God is nothing that could ever be named.

Tithing is necessary and you do tithe with God. *But from now on give to the only God and see to it that you give him the quality that you desire as man to express by claiming yourself to be the great, the wealthy, the loving, the all wise.*

Do not speculate as to how you shall express these qualities or claims, for life has a way that you, as man, know not of. Its ways are past finding out. But, I assure you, the day you claim these qualities to the point of conviction, your claims will be honored.

There is nothing covered that shall be uncovered. That which is spoken in secret shall be proclaimed from the housetops. *That is, your secret convictions of yourself—these secret claims that no man knows of, when really believed, will be shouted from the housetops in your world. For your convictions of yourself are the words of the God within you, which words are spirit and cannot return unto you void but must accomplish whereunto they are sent.*

You are at this moment calling out of the infinite that which you are now conscious of being. And not one word or conviction will fail to find you . . .

. . . To dissolve a problem that now seems so real to you all that you do is remove your attention from it. In spite of its seeming reality, turn from it in consciousness.

Become indifferent and begin to feel yourself to be that which would be the solution of the problem.

For instance; if you were imprisoned no man would have to tell you that you should desire freedom. Freedom, or rather the desire of freedom would be automatic. So why look behind the four walls of your prison bars? *Take your attention from being imprisoned and begin to feel yourself to be free. Feel it to the point where it is natural—the very second you do so, those prison bars will dissolve. Apply this same principle to any problem.*

CHAPTER 2

"The Secret of Feeling"

From *Freedom for All,* 1942

The secret of feeling or the calling of the invisible into visible states is beautifully told in the story of Isaac blessing his second son Jacob in the belief, based solely upon feeling, that he was blessing his first son Esau. It is recorded that Isaac, who was old and blind, felt that he was about to leave this world and wishing to bless his first son Esau before he died, sent Esau hunting for savory venison with the promise that upon his return from the hunt he would receive his father's blessing.

Now Jacob, who desired the birthright or right to be born through the blessing of his father, overheard his blind father's request for venison and his promise to Esau. So, as Esau went hunting for the venison, Jacob killed and dressed a kid of his father's flock. Placing the skins upon his smooth body to give him the feel of his hairy and rough brother Esau, he brought the tastily prepared kid to his blind father Isaac. And Isaac who depended solely upon his sense of feel mistook his second son Jacob for his first son Esau, and pronounced his blessing on Jacob! Esau on his return from the hunt learned that his smooth-skinned brother Jacob had supplanted him so he appealed to his father for justice; but Isaac answered and said, "Thy brother came with subtlety and hath taken away thy blessing. I have made him thy Lord, and all his brethren have I given to him for servants."

Simple human decency should tell man that this story cannot be taken literally. There must be a message for man hidden somewhere in this treacherous and despicable act of Jacob! The hidden message, the formula of success buried in this story was intuitively revealed to the writer in this manner. Isaac, the blind father, is your consciousness; your awareness of being. Esau, the hairy son, is your present objectified world—the rough or sensibly felt; the present moment; the present environment; your present conception of yourself; in short, the world you know by reason of your objective senses. Jacob, the smooth-skinned lad, the second son, is your desire or subjective state; an idea not yet embodied; a subjective state which is perceived and sensed but not objectively known or seen; a point in time and space removed from the pres-

ent. In short, Jacob is your defined objective. The smooth-skinned Jacob—or subjective state seeking embodiment or the right of birth—when properly felt or blessed by his father (when consciously felt and fixed as real), becomes objectified; and in so doing he supplants the rough, hairy Esau, or the former objectified state. Two things cannot occupy a given place at one and the same time, and so as the invisible is made visible, the former visible state vanishes.

Your consciousness is the cause of your world. The conscious state in which you abide determines the kind of world in which you live. Your present concept of yourself is now objectified as your environment, and this state is symbolized as Esau, the hairy, or sensibly felt; the first son. That which you would like to be or possess is symbolized as your second son, Jacob, the smooth-skinned lad who is not yet seen but is subjectively sensed and felt, and will, if properly touched, supplant his brother Esau, or your present world.

Always bear in mind the fact that Isaac, the father of these two sons, or states, is blind. He does not see his smooth-skinned son Jacob; he only feels him. And through the sense of feeling he actually believes Jacob, the subjective, to be Esau, the real, the objectified. You do not see your desire objectively; you simply sense it (feel it) subjectively. You do not grope in space after a desirable state. Like Isaac, you sit still and send your first son hunting by removing your attention from your objective world. Then in the absence of your first son, Esau, you invite the desirable state, your second son, Jacob, to come close so that you may feel it. "Come close, my son, that I may feel you." First, you are aware of it in your immediate environment; then you draw it closer and closer and closer until you sense it and feel it in your immediate presence so that it is real and natural to you.

"If two of you shall agree on earth as touching on any point that they shall ask, it shall be done for them of my Father which is in heaven." The two agree through the sense of feel; and the agreement is established on earth—is objectified; is made real. The two agreeing are Isaac and Jacob—you and that which you desire; and the agreement is made solely on the sense of feeling. Esau symbolizes your present objectified world whether it be pleasant or otherwise. Jacob symbolizes any and every desire of your heart. Isaac symbolizes your true self—with your eyes closed to the present world—in the act of sensing and feeling yourself to be or to possess that which you desire to be or to possess. The secret of Isaac—this sensing, feeling state—is simply the act of mentally separating the sensibly felt (your present physical state) from the insensibly felt (that which you would like to be). With the objective senses tightly shut Isaac made, and you can make the insensibly felt (the subjective state) seem real or sensibly known; for faith is knowledge.

Knowing the law of self-expression, the law by which the invisible is made visible, is not enough. It must be applied; and this is the method of application.

First: Send your first son Esau—your present objectified world or problem—hunting. This is accomplished simply by closing your eyes and taking your attention away from the objectified limitations. As your senses are removed from your objective world, it vanishes from your consciousness or goes hunting.

Second: With your eyes still closed and your attention removed from the world round about you, consciously fix the natural time and place for the realization of your desire.

With your objective senses closed to your present environment you can sense and feel the reality of any point in time or space, for both are psychological and can be created at will. It is vitally important that the natural time-space condition of Jacob, that is, the natural time and place for the realization of your desire be first fixed in your consciousness. If Sunday is the day on which the thing desired is to be realized, then Sunday must be fixed in consciousness now. Simply begin to feel that it is Sunday until the quietness and naturalness of Sunday is consciously established. You have definite associations with the days, weeks, months and seasons of the year. You have said time and again—"Today feels like Sunday, or Monday, or Saturday; or this feels like Spring, or Summer, or Fall, or Winter." This should convince you that you have definite, conscious impressions that you associate with the days, weeks, and seasons of the year. Then because of these associations you can select any desirable time, and by recalling the conscious impression associated with such time, you can make a subjective reality of that time now.

Do the same with space. If the room in which you are seated is not the room in which the thing desired would be naturally placed or realized, feel yourself seated in the room or place where it would be natural. Consciously fix this time-space impression before you start the act of sensing and feeling the nearness, the reality, and the possession of the thing desired. It matters not whether the place desired be ten thousand miles away or only next door, you must fix in consciousness the fact that right where you are seated is the desired place. You do not make a mental journey; you collapse space. Sit quietly where you are and make "thereness"—"hereness." Close your eyes and feel that the very place where you are is the place desired; feel and sense the reality of it until you are consciously impressed with this fact, for your knowledge of this fact is based solely on your subjective sensing.

Third: In the absence of Esau (the problem) and with the natural time-space established, you invite Jacob (the solution) to come and fill this space—to come and supplant his brother. In your imagination see the thing desired. If you cannot visualize it, sense the general outline of it; contemplate it. Then mentally draw it close to you. "Come close, my son, that I may feel you." Feel the nearness of it; feel it to be in your immediate presence; feel the reality and solidity of it; feel it and see it naturally placed in the room in which you are seated; feel the thrill of actual accomplishment, and the joy of possession.

Now open your eyes. This brings you back to the objective world—the rough or sensibly felt world. Your hairy son Esau has returned from the hunt and by his very presence tells you that you have been betrayed by your smooth-skinned son Jacob,—the subjective, psychologically felt. But, like Isaac, whose confidence was based upon the knowledge of this changeless law, you too will say—"I have made him thy Lord and all his brethren have I given to him for servants." That is, even though your problem appears fixed and real, you have felt the subjective, psychological state to be real to the point of receiving the thrill of that reality; you have experienced the secret of creation for you have felt the reality of the subjective.

You have fixed a definite psychological state which in spite of all opposition or precedent will objectify itself, thereby fulfilling the name of Jacob— the supplanter.

Here are a few practical examples of this drama.

First: The blessing or making a thing real. Sit in your living room and name a piece of furniture, rug or lamp that you would like to have in this particular room. Look at that area of the room where you would place it if you had it. Close your eyes and let all that now occupies that area of the room vanish. In your imagination see this area as empty space—there is absolutely nothing there. Now begin to fill this space with the desired piece of furniture; sense and feel that you have it in this very area. Imagine you are seeing that which you desired to see. Continue in this consciousness until you feel the thrill of possession.

Second: The blessing or the making of a place real. You are now seated in your apartment in New York City, contemplating the joy that would be yours if you were on an ocean liner sailing across the great Atlantic. "I go to prepare a place for you. And if I go and prepare a place for you,

*I will come again, and receive you unto myself:
that where I am there ye may be also." Your eyes
are closed; you have consciously released the New
York apartment and in its place you sense and feel
that you are on an ocean liner. You are seated in a
deck chair; there is nothing round you but the vast
Atlantic. Fix the reality of this ship and ocean so
that in this state you can mentally recall the day
when you were seated in your New York apartment
dreaming of this day at sea. Recall the mental picture of yourself seated there in New York dreaming
of this day. In your imagination see the memory
picture of your-self back there in your New York
apartment. If you succeed in looking back on your
New York apartment without consciously returning there, then you have successfully prepared the
reality of this voyage. Remain in this conscious
state feeling the reality of the ship and the ocean;
feel the joy of this accomplishment—then open
your eyes. You have gone and prepared the place;
you have fixed a definite psychological state and
where you are in consciousness there you shall be
in body also.*

*Third: The blessing or making real of a point
in time. You consciously let go of this day, month
or year, as the case may be, and you imagine that
it is now that day, month or year which you desire
to experience. You sense and feel the reality of the*

desired time by impressing upon yourself the fact that it is now accomplished. As you sense the naturalness of this time, you begin to feel the thrill of having fully realized that which before you started this psychological journey in time you desired to experience at this time.

With the knowledge of your power to bless you can open the doors of any prison—the prison of illness or poverty or of a humdrum existence. "The Spirit of the Lord God is upon me; because the Lord hath anointed me to preach good tidings unto the meek; he hath sent me to bind up the brokenhearted, to proclaim liberty to the captives, and the opening of the prison to them that are bound."

CHAPTER 3

"Sleep"

From *Feeling Is the Secret*, 1944

Sleep, the life that occupies one-third of our stay on earth, is the natural door into the subconscious. So it is with sleep that we are now concerned. The conscious two-thirds of our life on earth is measured by the degree of attention we give sleep. Our understanding of and delight in what sleep has to bestow will cause us, night after night, to set out for it as though we were keeping an appointment with a lover.

"In a dream, in a vision of the night, when deep sleep falleth upon men, in slumbering upon the bed; then he openeth the ears of men and sealeth their instruction." Job 33. It is in sleep and in prayer, a state akin to sleep, that man enters the subconscious to make his impressions and receive his instructions. In these states the conscious and subconscious are creatively joined. The male and female become one flesh.

Sleep is the time when the male or conscious mind turns from the world of sense to seek its lover or subconscious self. The subconscious—unlike the woman of the world who marries her husband to change him—has no desire to change the conscious, waking state, but loves it as it is and faithfully reproduces its likeness in the outer world of form. The conditions and events of your life are your children formed from the molds of your subconscious impressions in sleep. They are made in the image and likeness of your innermost feeling that they may reveal you to yourself.

"As in heaven so on earth." As in the subconscious so on earth. Whatever you have in consciousness as you go to sleep is the measure of your expression in the waking two-thirds of your life on earth. Nothing stops you from realizing your objective save your failure to feel that you are already that which you wish to be, or that you are already in possession of the thing sought. Your subconscious gives form to your desires only when you feel your wish fulfilled.

The unconsciousness of sleep is the normal state of the subconscious. Because all things come from within yourself, and your conception of yourself determines that which comes, you should always feel the wish fulfilled before you drop off to sleep.

You never draw out of the deep of yourself that which you want; you always draw that which you are, and you are that which you feel yourself to be as well as that which you feel as true of others.

To be realized, then, the wish must be resolved into the feeling of being or having or witnessing the state sought. This is accomplished by assuming the feeling of the wish fulfilled. The feeling which comes in response to the question "How would I feel were my wish realized?" is the feeling which should monopolize and immobilize your attention as you relax into sleep. You must be in the consciousness of being or having that which you want to be or to have before you drop off to sleep.

Once asleep man has no freedom of choice. His entire slumber is dominated by his last waking concept of self. It follows, therefore, that *he should always assume the feeling of accomplishment and satisfaction before he retires in sleep.* "Come before me with singing and thanksgiving." "Enter into his gates with thanksgiving and into his courts with praise." Your mood prior to sleep defines your state of consciousness as you enter into the presence of your everlasting lover, the subconscious. She sees you exactly as you feel yourself to be. If, as you prepare for sleep, you assume and maintain the consciousness of success by feeling "I am successful," you must be successful. Lie flat on your back with your head on a level with your body. Feel as you would were you in possession of your wish and quietly relax into unconsciousness.

"He that keepeth Israel shall neither slumber nor sleep." Nevertheless "He giveth his beloved sleep." The subconscious never sleeps. Sleep is the door through which the conscious, waking mind passes to be creatively joined to the subconscious. Sleep conceals the creative act while the objective world reveals it. In sleep man impresses the subconscious with his conception of himself...

...*Preparing to sleep, you feel yourself into the state of the answered wish, and then relax into unconsciousness.* Your realized wish is he whom you seek. By night on your bed you seek the feeling of the wish fulfilled that you may take it with you into the chamber of her that conceived you, into sleep or the subconscious which gave you form, that this wish also may be given expression. This is the way to discover and conduct your wishes into the subconscious. *Feel yourself in the state of the realized wish and quietly drop off to sleep.*

Night after night you should assume the feeling of being, having and witnessing that which you seek to be, possess and see manifested. Never go to sleep feeling discouraged or dissatisfied. Never sleep in the consciousness of failure. Your subconscious, whose natural state is sleep, sees you as you believe yourself to be, and whether it be good, bad, or indifferent, the subconscious will faithfully embody your belief. As you feel so do you impress her; and she, the perfect lover, gives form to these impressions and out pictures them as the children of her beloved.

"Thou art all fair, my love; there is no spot in thee," is the attitude of mind to adopt before dropping off to sleep. *Disregard appearances and feel that things are as you wish them to be*, for "He calleth things that are not seen as though they were, and the unseen becomes seen." To assume the feeling of satisfaction is to call conditions into being which will mirror satisfaction. "Signs follow, they do not precede." *Proof that you are will follow the consciousness that you are; it will not precede it.*

You are an eternal dreamer dreaming non-eternal dreams. Your dreams take form as you assume the feeling of their reality. Do not limit yourself to the past. Knowing that nothing is impossible to consciousness begin to imagine states beyond the experiences of the past. Whatever the mind of man can imagine man can realize. All objective (visible) states were first subjective (invisible) states, and you called them into visible states by assuming the feeling of their reality. The creative process is first imagining and then believing the state imagined. Always imagine and expect the best.

The world cannot change until you change your conception of it. "As within so without." Nations as well as people are only what you believe them to be. No matter what the problem is, no matter where it is, no matter whom it concerns, you have no one to change but yourself, and you have neither opponent nor helper in bringing about the change within yourself. You have nothing to do but convince yourself of the truth of that which you desire to see manifested. As soon as you succeed in convincing yourself of the reality of the state sought, results follow to confirm your fixed belief. You never suggest to another the state which you desire to see him express; instead you convince yourself that he is already that which you desire him to be.

Realization of your wish is accomplished by assuming the feeling of the wish fulfilled. You cannot fail unless you fail to convince yourself of the reality of your wish. A change of belief is confirmed by a change of expression. *Every night as you drop off to sleep feel satisfied and spotless, for your subjective lover always forms the objective world in the image and likeness of your conception of it, the conception defined by your feeling.*

The waking two-thirds of your life on earth ever corroborates or bears witness to your subconscious impressions. The actions and events of the day are effects; they are not causes. Free will is only freedom of choice. "Choose ye this day whom ye shall serve" is your freedom to choose the kind of mood you assume; but the expression of the mood is the secret of the subconscious. *The subconscious receives impressions only through the feelings of man and in a way known only to itself gives these impressions form and expression. The actions of man are determined by his subconscious impressions. His illusion of free will, his belief in freedom of action, is but ignorance of the causes which make him act. He thinks himself free because he has forgotten the link between himself and the event.*

Man awake is under compulsion to express his subconscious impressions. If in the past he unwisely impressed himself, then let him begin to change his thought and feeling, for only as he does so will he change his world. *Do not waste one moment in regret, for to think feelingly of the mistakes of the past is to reinfect yourself.* "Let the dead bury the dead." Turn from appearances and assume the feeling that would be yours were you already the one you wish to be.

Feeling a state produces that state. The part you play on the world's stage is determined by your conception of yourself. By feeling your wish fulfilled and quietly relaxing into sleep, you cast yourself in a star role to be played on earth tomorrow, and while asleep you are rehearsed and instructed in your part.

The acceptance of the end automatically wills the means of realization. Make no mistake about this. If, as you prepare for sleep, you do not consciously feel yourself into the state of the answered wish, then you will take with you into the chamber of her who conceived you the sum total of the reactions and feelings of the waking day; and while asleep you will be instructed in the manner in which they will be expressed tomorrow. You will rise believing that you are a free agent, not realizing that every action and event of the day is predetermined by your concept of self as you fell asleep. Your only freedom then is your freedom of reaction. You are free to choose how you feel and react to the day's drama, but the drama—the actions, events and circumstances of the day—have already been determined.

Unless you consciously and purposely define the attitude of mind with which you go to sleep, you unconsciously go to sleep in the composite attitude of mind made up of all feelings and reactions of the day. Every reaction makes a subconscious impression and, unless counteracted by an opposite and more dominant feeling, is the cause of future action.

Ideas enveloped in feeling are creative actions. Use your divine right wisely. Through your ability to think and feel you have dominion over all creation.

While you are awake you are a gardener selecting seed for your garden, but "Except a corn of wheat fall into the ground and die, it abideth alone; but if it die, it bringeth forth much fruit." *Your conception of yourself as you fall asleep is the seed you drop into the ground of the subconscious. Dropping off to sleep feeling satisfied and happy compels conditions and events to appear in your world which confirm these attitudes of mind.*

Sleep is the door into heaven. What you take in as a feeling you bring out as a condition, action, or object in space. So sleep in the feeling of the wish fulfilled. "As in consciousness so on earth."

CHAPTER 4

"Prayer: The Art of Believing"

1945

Preface

Prayer is the master key. A key may fit one door of a house, but when it fits all doors it may well claim to be a master key. Such and no less a key is prayer to all earthly problems.

Chapter 1
LAW OF REVERSIBILITY

"Pray for my soul, more things are wrought by prayer than this world dreams of."
—Tennyson

Prayer is an art and requires practice. The first requirement is a controlled imagination. Parade and vain repetitions are foreign to prayer. Its exercise requires tranquility and peace of mind, "Use not vain repetitions," for prayer is done in secret and "thy Father which seeth in secret shall reward thee openly." The ceremonies that are customarily used in prayer are mere superstitions and have been invented to give prayer an air of solemnity. Those who do practice the art of prayer are often ignorant of the laws that control it. They attribute the results obtained to the ceremonies and mistake the letter for the spirit. The essence of prayer is faith; but faith must be permeated with understanding to be given that active quality which it does not possess when standing alone. "Therefore, get wisdom; and with all thy getting get understanding."

This book is an attempt to reduce the unknown to the known, by pointing out the conditions on which prayers are answered, and without which they cannot be answered. It defines the conditions governing prayer in laws that are simply a generalization of our observations.

The universal law of reversibility is the foundation on which its claims are based.

Mechanical motion caused by speech was known for a long time before anyone dreamed of the possibility of an inverse transformation, that is, the reproduction of speech by mechanical motion (the phonograph). For a long time electricity was produced by friction without ever a thought that friction, in turn, could be produced by electricity.

Whether or not man succeeds in reversing the transformation of a force, he knows, nevertheless, that all transformations of force are reversible. If heat can produce mechanical motion, so mechanical motion can produce heat. If electricity produces magnetism, magnetism too can develop electric currents. If the voice can cause undulatory currents, so can such currents reproduce the voice, and so on. Cause and effect, energy and matter, action and reaction are the same and inter-convertible.

This law is of the highest importance, because it enables you to foresee the inverse transformation once the direct transformation is verified. If you knew how you would feel were you to realize your objective, then, inversely, you would know what state you could realize were you to awaken in yourself such feeling. The injunction, to pray believing that you already possess what you pray for, is based upon a knowledge of the law of inverse transformation. If your realized prayer produces in you a definite feeling or state of consciousness, then, inversely, that particular feeling or state of consciousness must produce your realized prayer. *Because all transformations of force are reversible, you should always assume the feeling of your fulfilled wish. You should awaken within you the feeling that you are and have that which heretofore you desired to be and possess. This is easily done by contemplat-*

ing the joy that would be yours were your objective an accomplished fact, so that you live and move and have your being in the feeling that your wish is realized.

The feeling of the wish fulfilled, if assumed and sustained, must objectify the state that would have created it. This law explains why "Faith is the substance of things hoped for, the evidence of things not seen" and why "He calleth things that are not seen as though they were and things that were not seen become seen." Assume the feeling of your wish fulfilled and continue feeling that it is fulfilled until that which you feel objectifies itself.

If a physical fact can produce a psychological state, a psychological state can produce a physical fact. If the effect (a) can be produced by the cause (b), then inversely, the effect (b) can be produced by the cause (a). Therefore I say unto you, "What things soever ye desire, when ye pray, believe that ye have received them, and ye shall have them" (Mark 11:24, E.R.V.).

Chapter 2
DUAL NATURE OF CONSCIOUSNESS

A clear concept of the dual nature of man's consciousness must be the basis of all true prayer. Consciousness includes a subconscious as well as a conscious part. The infinitely greater part of consciousness lies below the sphere of objective consciousness. The subconscious is the most important part of consciousness. It is the cause of voluntary action. The subconscious is what a man is. The conscious is what a man knows. "I and my Father are one but my Father is greater than I." The conscious and subconscious are one, but the subconscious is greater than the conscious.

"I of myself can do nothing, the Father within me He doeth the work." I, objective consciousness, of myself can do nothing; the Father, the subconscious, He doeth the work. The subconscious is that in which everything is known, in which everything is possible, to which everything goes, from which everything comes, which belongs to all, to which all have access.

What we are conscious of is constructed out of what we are not conscious of. Not only do our subconscious assumptions influence our behavior but they also fashion the pattern of our objective existence. They alone have the power to say, "Let us make man—objective manifestations—in our image, after our likeness." The whole of creation is asleep within the deep of man and is awakened to objective existence by his subconscious assumptions. Within that blankness we call sleep there is a consciousness in unsleeping vigilance, and while the body sleeps this unsleeping being releases from the treasure house of eternity the subconscious assumptions of man.

Prayer is the key which unlocks the infinite storehouse. "Prove me now herewith, saith the Lord of hosts, if I will not open you the windows of heaven, and pour you out a blessing, that there shall not be room enough to receive it." Prayer modifies or completely changes our subconscious assumptions, and *a change of assumption is a change of expression.*

The conscious mind reasons inductively from observation, experience and education. It therefore finds it difficult to believe what the five senses and inductive reason deny. The subconscious reasons deductively and is never concerned with the truth or falsity of the premise, but proceeds on the assumption of the correctness of the premise and objectifies results which are consistent with the premise. This distinction must be clearly seen by all who would master the art of praying. No true grasp of the science of prayer can be really obtained until the laws governing the dual nature of consciousness are understood and the importance of the subconscious realized.

Prayer—the art of believing what is denied by the senses—deals almost entirely with the subconscious. Through prayer, the subconscious is suggested into acceptance of the wish fulfilled, and, reasoning deductively, logically unfolds it to its legitimate end. "Far greater is He that is in you than he that is in the world."

The subjective mind is the diffused consciousness that animates the world; it is the spirit that giveth life. In all substance is a single soul—subjective mind. Through all creation runs this one unbroken subjective mind. *Thought and feeling fused into beliefs impress modifications upon it, charge it with a mission, which mission it faithfully executes.*

The conscious mind originates premises. The subjective mind unfolds them to their logical ends. Were the subjective mind not so limited in its initiative power of reasoning, objective man could not be held responsible for his actions in the world. Man transmits ideas to the subconscious through his feelings. The subconscious transmits ideas from mind to mind through telepathy. Your unexpressed convictions of others are transmitted to them without their conscious knowledge or consent, and if subconsciously accepted by them will influence their behavior.

The only ideas they subconsciously reject are your ideas of them which they could not wish to be true of anyone. Whatever they could wish for others can be believed of them, and by the law of belief which governs subjective reasoning they are compelled to subjectively accept, and therefore objectively express, accordingly.

The subjective mind is completely controlled by suggestion. Ideas are best suggested when the objective mind is partly subjective, that is, when the objective senses are diminished or held in abeyance. This partly subjective state can best be described as controlled reverie, wherein the mind is passive but capable of functioning with absorption. It is a concentration of attention. There must be no conflict in your mind when you are praying. Turn from what is to what ought to be. *Assume the mood of fulfilled desire, and by the universal law of reversibility you will realize your desire.*

Chapter 3
IMAGINATION AND FAITH

Prayers are not successfully made unless there is rapport between the conscious and subconscious mind of the operator. This is done through imagination and faith.

By the power of imagination all men, certainly imaginative men, are forever casting forth enchantments, and all men, especially unimaginative men, are continually passing under their power. Can we ever be certain that it was not our mother while darning our socks who began that subtle change in our minds? *If I can unintentionally cast an enchantment over persons, there is no reason to doubt that I am able to cast intentionally a far stronger enchantment.*

Everything, that can be seen, touched, explained, argued over, is to the imaginative man nothing more than a means, for he functions, by reason of his controlled imagination, in the deep of himself where every idea exists in itself and not in relation to something else. In him there is no need for the restraints of reason, for the only restraint he can obey is the mysterious instinct that teaches him to eliminate all moods other than the mood of fulfilled desire.

Imagination and faith are the only faculties of mind needed to create objective conditions. The faith required for the successful operation of the law of consciousness is a purely subjective faith and is attainable upon the cessation of active opposition on the part of the objective mind of the operator. It depends upon your ability to feel and accept as true what your objective senses deny. Neither the passivity of the subject nor his conscious agreement with your suggestion is necessary, for without his consent or knowledge he can be given a subjective order which he must objectively express. It is a fundamental law of consciousness that by telepathy we can have immediate communion with another.

To establish rapport you call the subject mentally. Focus your attention on him and mentally shout his name just as you would to attract the attention of anyone. Imagine that he has answered, and mentally hear his voice. Represent him to yourself inwardly in the state you want him to obtain. Then imagine that he is telling you in the tones of ordinary conversation what you want to hear. Mentally answer him. Tell him of your joy in witnessing his good fortune. Having mentally heard with all the distinctness of reality that which you wanted to hear, and having thrilled to the news heard, return to objective consciousness. Your subjective conversation must awaken what it affirmed.

"Thou shalt decree a thing and it shall be established unto thee." It is not a strong will that sends the subjective word on its mission so much as it is clear thinking and feeling the truth of the state affirmed. When belief and will are in conflict, belief invariably wins. "Not by might, nor by power, but by my spirit, saith the Lord of hosts." It is not what you want that you attract; you attract what you believe to be true. Therefore, get into the spirit of these mental conversations and give them the same degree of reality that you would a telephone conversation. "If thou canst believe, all things are possible to him that believeth. Therefore, I say unto you, what things soever ye desire, when ye pray, believe that ye have received them, and ye shall have them." The acceptance of the end wills the means. And the wisest reflection could not devise more effective means than those which are willed by the acceptance of the end. *Mentally talk to your friends as though your desires for them were already realized.*

Imagination is the beginning of the growth of all forms, and faith is the substance out of which they are formed. By imagination, that which exists in latency or is asleep within the deep of consciousness is awakened and is given a form. The cures attributed to the influence of certain medicines, relics and places are the effects of imagination and faith. The curative power is not in the spirit that is in them, it is in the spirit in which they are accepted. "The letter killeth, but the spirit giveth life."

The subjective mind is completely controlled by suggestion, so, whether the object of your faith be true or false, you will get the same results. There is nothing unsound in the theory of medicine or in the claims of the priesthood for their relics and holy places.

The subjective mind of the patient accepts the suggestion of health conditioned on such states, and as soon as these conditions are met proceeds to realize health. "According to your faith be it done unto you for all things are possible to him that believeth." Confident expectation of a state is the most potent means of bringing it about. The confident expectation of a cure does that which no medical treatment can accomplish.

Failure is always due to an antagonistic auto-suggestion by the patient, arising from objective doubt of the power of the medicine or relic, or from doubt of the truth of the theory. Many of us, either from too little emotion or too much intellect, both of which are stumbling blocks in the way of prayer, cannot believe that which our senses deny. To force ourselves to believe will end in greater doubt. To avoid such counter-suggestions the patient should be unaware, objectively, of the suggestions which are made to him. *The most effective method of healing or influencing the behavior of others consists in what is known as "the silent or absent treatment." When the subject is unaware, objectively, of the suggestion given him there is no possibility of him setting up an antagonistic belief. It is not necessary that the patient know, objectively, that anything is being done for him. From what is known of the subjective and objective processes of reasoning, it is better that he should not know objectively of that which is being done for him. The more completely the objective mind is kept in ignorance of the suggestion, the better will the subjective mind perform its functions. The subject subconsciously accepts the suggestion and thinks he originates it, proving the truth of Spinoza's dictum that we know not the causes that determine our actions.*

The subconscious mind is the universal conductor which the operator modifies with his thoughts and feelings. Visible states are either the vibratory effects of subconscious vibrations within you or they are the vibratory causes of corresponding vibrations within you. A disciplined man never permits them to be causes unless they awaken in him desirable states of consciousness. With a knowledge of the law of reversibility, the disciplined man transforms his world by imagining and feeling only what is lovely and of good report. The beautiful idea he awakens within himself shall not fail to arouse its affinity in others. He knows the savior of the world is not a man but the manifestation that would save. The sick man's savior is health, the hungry man's savior is food, the thirsty man's savior is water. He walks in the company of the savior by assuming the feeling of his wish fulfilled. By the laws of reversibility, that all transformations of force are reversible, the energy or feeling awakened transforms itself into the state imagined. He never waits four months for the harvest. If in four months the harvest will awaken in him a state of joy, then, inversely, the joy of harvest now will awaken the harvest now. "Now is the acceptable time to give beauty for ashes, joy for mourning, praise for the spirit of heaviness; that they might be called trees of righteousness, the planting of the Lord that he might be glorified."

Chapter 4
CONTROLLED REVERIE

Everyone is amenable to the same psychological laws which govern the ordinary hypnotic subject. He is amenable to control by suggestion. In hypnosis, the objective senses are partly or totally suspended. However, no matter how profoundly the objective senses are locked in hypnosis, the subjective faculties are alert, and the subject recognizes everything that goes on around him. The activity and power of the subjective mind are proportionate to the sleep of the objective mind. Suggestions which appear powerless when presented directly to objective consciousness are highly efficacious when the subject is in the hypnotic state. The hypnotic state is simply being unaware, objectively. In hypnotism, the conscious mind is put to sleep and the subconscious powers are exposed so as to be directly reached by suggestion. It is easy to see from this, providing you accept the truth of mental suggestions, that anyone not objectively aware of you is in a profound hypnotic state relative to you. Therefore, "Curse not the king, no not in thy thought; and curse not the rich in thy bedchamber; for a bird of the air shall carry the voice, and that which hath wings shall tell the matter" (Ecc. 10:20). What you sincerely believe as true of another you awaken within him.

No one need be entranced, in the ordinary manner, to be helped. If the subject is consciously unaware of the suggestion, and if the suggestion is given with conviction and confidently accepted by the operator as true, then you have the ideal setting for a successful prayer. Represent the subject to yourself mentally as though he had already done that which you desire him to do. Mentally speak to him and congratulate him on having done what you want him to do. Mentally see him in the state you want him to obtain. Within the circle of its action, every word subjectively spoken awakens, objectively, what it affirms. Incredulity on the part of the subject is no hindrance when you are in control of your reverie.

Bold assertion by you, while you are in a partly subjective state, awakens what you affirm. Self-confidence on your part and the thorough belief in the truth of your mental assertion are all that is needed to produce results. Visualize the subject and imagine that you hear his voice. This establishes contact with his subjective mind. Then imagine that he is telling you what you want to hear. If you want to send him words of health and wealth, then imagine that he is telling you, "I have never felt better and I have never had more," and mentally tell him of your joy in witnessing his good fortune. Imagine that you see and hear his joy.

A mental conversation with the subjective image of another must be in a manner which does not express the slightest doubt as to the truth of what you hear and say. If you have the least idea that you do not believe what you have imagined you have heard and seen, the subject will not comply, for your subjective mind will transmit only your fixed ideas. Only fixed ideas can awaken their vibratory correlates in those toward whom they are directed. In the controlled reverie, ideas must be suggested with the utmost care. If you do not control your imagination in the reverie, your imagination will control you. Whatever you suggest with confidence is law to the subjective mind; it is under obligation to objectify that which you mentally affirm. Not only does the subject execute the state affirmed but he does it as though the decision had come of itself, or the idea had been originated by him.

Control of the subconscious is dominion over all. Each state obeys one mind's control. Control of the subconscious is accomplished through control of your beliefs, which in turn is the all-potent factor in the production of visible states. Imagination and faith are the secrets of creation.

Chapter 5
LAW OF THOUGHT TRANSMISSION

"He sent his word and healed them, and delivered them from their destructions." He transmitted the consciousness of health and it awoke its vibratory correlate in the one toward whom it was directed. He mentally represented the subject to himself in a state of health and imagined he heard the subject confirm it. "For no word of God shall be void of power; therefore hold fast the pattern of healthful words which thou hast heard."

To pray successfully you must have clearly defined objectives. You must know what you want before you can ask for it. You must know what you want before you can feel that you have it, and prayer is the feeling of fulfilled desire. It does not matter what it is you seek in prayer, or where it is, or whom it concerns. You have nothing to do but convince yourself of the truth of that which you desire to see manifested. When you emerge from prayer you no longer seek, for you have—if you have prayed correctly—subconsciously assumed the reality of the state sought, and by the law of reversibility your subconscious assumption must objectify that which it affirms.

You must have a conductor to transmit a force. You may employ a wire, a jet of water, a current of air, a ray of light or any intermediary whatsoever. The principle of the photophone or the transmission of voice by light will help you to understand thought transmission, or the sending of a word to heal another. *There is a strong analogy between a spoken voice and a mental voice. To think is to speak low, to speak is to think aloud.* The principle of the photophone is this: A ray of light is reflected by a mirror and projected to a receiver at a distant point. Back of the mirror is a mouthpiece. By speaking into the mouthpiece you cause the mirror to vibrate. A vibrating mirror modifies the light reflected on it. The modified light has your speech to carry, not as speech, but as represented in its mechanical correlate. It reaches the distant station and impinges on a disk within the receiver; it causes the disk to vibrate according to the modification it undergoes— and it reproduces your voice.

"I am the light of the world." I am, the knowledge that I exist, is a light by means of which what passes in my mind is rendered visible. Memory, or my ability to mentally see what is not objectively present, proves that my mind is a mirror, and so sensitive a mirror that it can reflect a thought. The reperception of an image in memory in no way differs as a visual act from the perception of my image in a mirror. The same principle of seeing is involved in both.

Your consciousness is the light reflected on the mirror of your mind and projected in space to the one of whom you think. By mentally speaking to the subjective image in your mind you cause the mirror of your mind to vibrate. Your vibrating mind modifies the light of consciousness reflected on it. The modified light of consciousness reaches the one toward whom it is directed and impinges on the mirror of his mind; it causes his mind to vibrate according to the modifications it undergoes. Thus, it reproduces in him what was mentally affirmed by you.

Your beliefs, your fixed attitudes of mind, constantly modify your consciousness as it is reflected on the mirror of your mind. Your consciousness, modified by your beliefs, objectifies itself in the conditions of your world. To change the world, you must first change your conception of it. To change a man, you must change your conception of him. You must believe him to be the man you want him to be and mentally talk to him as though he were. All men are sufficiently sensitive to reproduce your beliefs of them. Therefore, if your word is not reproduced visibly in him toward whom it is sent, the cause is to be found in you, not in the subject. As soon as you believe in the truth of the state affirmed, results follow. Everyone can be transformed; every thought can be transmitted; every thought can be visibly embodied.

Subjective words—subconscious assumptions—awaken what they affirm. "They are living and active and shall not return unto me void, but shall accomplish that which I please, and shall prosper in the thing whereto I sent them." They are endowed with the intelligence pertaining to their mission and will persist until the object of their existence is realized; they persist until they awaken the vibratory correlates of themselves within the one toward whom they are directed, but the moment the object of their creation is accomplished they cease to be. The word spoken subjectively in quiet confidence will always awaken a corresponding state in the one for whom it was spoken; but the moment its task is accomplished it ceases to be, permitting the one in whom the state is realized to remain in the consciousness of the state affirmed or to return to his former state.

Whatever state has your attention holds your life. Therefore, to become attentive to a former state is to return to that condition. "Remember not the former things, neither consider the things of old."

—2—

Nothing can be added to man, for the whole of creation is already perfected within him. "The kingdom of heaven is within you." "Man can receive nothing, except it be given him from heaven." Heaven is your subconsciousness. Not even a sunburn is given from without. The rays without only awaken corresponding rays within. Were the burning rays not contained within man, all the concentrated rays in the universe could not burn him. Were the tones of health not contained within the consciousness of the one of whom they are affirmed, they could not be vibrated by the word which is sent. You do not really give to another—you resurrect that which is asleep within him. "The damsel is not dead, but sleepeth." Death is merely a sleeping and a forgetting. Age and decay are the sleep—not death—of youth and health. Recognition of a state vibrates or awakens it.

Distance, as it is cognized by your objective senses, does not exist for the subjective mind. "If I take the wings of the morning, and dwell in the uttermost parts of the sea; even there shall thy hand lead me." *Time and space are conditions of thought; the imagination can transcend them and move in a psychological time and space.* Although physically separated from a place by thousands of miles, you can mentally live in the distant place as though it were here. Your imagination can easily transform winter into summer, New York into Florida, and so on. Whether the object of your desire be near or far, results will be the same. *Subjectively, the object of your desire is never far off; its intense nearness makes it remote from observation of the*

senses. It dwells in consciousness, and conscious-
ness is closer than breathing and nearer than
hands and feet.

Consciousness is the one and only reality. All phenomena are formed of the same substance vibrating
at different rates. All is consciousness modified by
belief. Out of consciousness I as man came, and to
consciousness I as man return. In consciousness all
states exist subjectively, and are awakened to their
objective existence by belief. The only thing that
prevents us from making a successful subjective
impression on one at a great distance, or transforming there into here, is our habit of regarding space as
an obstacle.

A friend a thousand miles away is rooted in your
consciousness through your fixed ideas of him. To
think of him and represent him to yourself inwardly
in the state you desire him to be, confident that this
subjective image is as true as though it were already
objectified, awakens in him a corresponding state
which he must objectify. The results will be as
obvious as the cause was hidden. The subject will
express the awakened state within him and remain
unaware of the true cause of his action. Your illusion of free will is but ignorance of the causes which
make you act. Prayers depend upon your attitude
of mind for their success and not upon the attitude
of the subject. The subject has no power to resist

your controlled subjective ideas of him unless the state affirmed by you to be true of him is a state he is incapable of wishing as true of another. In that case, it returns to you, the sender, and will realize itself in you. Provided the idea is acceptable, success depends entirely on the operator not upon the subjects who, like compass needles on their pivots, are quite indifferent as to what direction you choose to give them. If your fixed idea is not subjectively accepted by the one toward whom it is directed, it rebounds to you from whom it came. "Who is he that will harm you, if ye be followers of that which is good? I have been young, and now am old; yet have I not seen the righteous forsaken, nor his seed begging bread." "There shall no evil happen to the just." Nothing befalls us that is not of the nature of ourselves.

A person who directs a malicious thought to another will be injured by its rebound if he fails to get subconscious acceptance of the other. "As ye sow, so shall ye reap." *Furthermore, what you can wish and believe of another can be wished and believed of you, and you have no power to reject it if the one who desires it for you accepts it as true of you. The only power to reject a subjective word is to be incapable of wishing a similar state of another—to give presupposes the ability to receive. The possibility to impress an idea upon another mind presupposes the ability of that mind to receive that impression. Fools exploit the world; the wise transfigure it.* It is the highest wisdom to know that in the living universe there is no destiny other than that created out of the imagination of man. There is no influence outside of the mind of man.

"Whatsoever things are lovely, whatsoever things are of good report; if there be any virtue, and if there be any praise, think on these things." *Never accept as true of others what you would not want to be true of you. To awaken a state within another it first must be awake within you.* The state you would transmit to another can be transmitted only if it is believed by you. Therefore, to give is to receive. *You cannot give what you do not have and you have only what you believe. So to believe a state as true of another not only awakens that state within the other but it makes it alive within you. You are what you believe.*

"Give and ye shall receive, full measure, pressed down and running over." Giving is simply believing, for what you truly believe of others you awaken within them. The vibratory state transmitted by your belief persists until it awakens its corresponding vibration in him of whom it is believed. But before it can be transmitted it must first be awake within the consciousness of the transmitter. Whatever is awake within your consciousness, you are. Whether the belief pertains to self or another does not matter, for the believer is defined by the sum total of his beliefs or subconscious assumptions.

"As a man thinketh in his heart"—in the deep subconscious of himself—"so is he." Disregard appearances and subjectively affirm as true that which you wish to be true. This awakens in you the tone of the state affirmed which in turn realizes itself in you and in the one of whom it is affirmed. Give and ye shall receive. Beliefs invariably awaken what they affirm. The world is a mirror wherein everyone sees himself reflected. The objective world reflects the beliefs of the subjective mind.

Some people are self-impressed best by visual images, others by mental sounds, and still others by mental actions. The form of mental activity which allows the whole power of your attention to be focused in one chosen direction is the one to cultivate, until you can bring all to play on your objective at the same time.

Should you have some difficulty in understanding the terms, "visual images," "mental sounds" and "mental actions," here is an illustration that should make their meanings clear: A imagines he sees a piece of music, knowing nothing at all about musical notations. The impression in his mind is a purely visual image. B imagines he sees the same piece, but he can read music and can imagine how it would sound when played on the piano; that imagination is mental sound. C also reads music and is a pianist; as he reads, he imagines himself playing the piece. The imaginary action is mental action.

The visual images, mental sounds and mental actions are creations of your imagination, and though they appear to come from without, they actually come from within yourself. They move as if moved by another but are really launched by your own spirit from the magical storehouse of imagination. They are projected into space by the same vibratory law that governs the sending of a voice or picture. Speech and images are projected not as speech or images but as vibratory correlates. Subjective mind vibrates according to the modifications it undergoes by the thought and feelings of the operator. The visible state created is the effect of the subjective vibrations. A feeling is always accompanied by a corresponding vibration, that is, a change in expression or sensation in the operator.

There is no thought or feeling without expression. No matter how motionless you appear to be if you reflect with any degree of intensity, there is always an execution of slight muscular movements. The eye, though shut, follows the movements of the imaginary objects and the pupil is dilated or contracted according to the brightness or the remoteness of those objects; respiration is accelerated or slowed, according to the course of your thoughts; the muscles contract correspondingly to your mental movements.

This change of vibration persists until it awakens a corresponding vibration in the subject, which vibration then expresses itself in a physical fact. "And the word was made flesh." Energy, as you see in the case of radio, is transmitted and received in a "field," a place where changes in space occur. The field and energy are one and inseparable. The field or subject becomes the embodiment of the word or energy received. The thinker and the thought, the operator and the subject, the energy and the field are one. Were you still enough to hear the sound of your beliefs you would know what is meant by "the music of the spheres." The mental sounds you hear in prayer as coming from without are really produced by yourself. Self-observation will reveal this fact. As the music of the spheres is defined as the harmony heard by the gods alone, and is supposed to be produced by the movements of the celestial spheres, so, too, is the harmony you subjectively hear for others heard by you alone and is produced by the movements of your thoughts and feelings in the true kingdom or "heaven within you."

Chapter 6
GOOD TIDINGS

*"How beautiful upon the mountains are the feet
of him that bringeth good tidings, that publisheth
peace, that bringeth good tidings of good,
that publisheth salvation."*

A very effective way to bring good tidings to another is to call before your mind's eye the subjective image of the person you wish to help and have him affirm that he has done that which you desired him to do. Mentally hear him tell you that he has done it. This awakens within him the vibratory correlate of the state affirmed, which vibration persists until its mission is accomplished. It does not matter what it is you desire to have done, or whom you select to do it. As soon as you subjectively affirm that it is done, results follow. Failure can result only if you fail to accept the truth of your assertion or if the state affirmed would not be desired by the subject for himself or another. In the latter event, the state would realize itself in you, the operator.

The seemingly harmless habit of "talking to yourself" is the most fruitful form of prayer. A mental argument with the subjective image of another is the surest way to pray for an argument. You are asking to be offended by the other when you objectively meet. He is compelled to act in a manner displeasing to you, unless before the meeting you countermand or modify your order by subjectively affirming a change.

Unfortunately, man forgets his subjective arguments, his daily mental conversations with others, and so is at a loss for an explanation of the conflicts and misfortunes of his life. As mental arguments produce conflicts, so happy mental conversations produce corresponding visible states of good tidings. Man creates himself out of his own imagination.

If the state desired is for yourself, and you find it difficult to accept as true what your senses deny, call before your mind's eye the subjective image of a friend and have him mentally affirm that you are already that which you desire to be. This establishes in him, without his conscious consent or knowledge, the subconscious assumption that you are that which he mentally affirmed, which assumption, because it is unconsciously assumed, will persist until it fulfills its mission. Its mission is to awaken in you its vibratory correlate, which vibration when awakened in you realizes itself as an objective fact.

Another very effective way to pray for oneself is to use the formula of Job who found that his own captivity was removed as he prayed for his friends. Fix your attention on a friend and have the imaginary voice of your friend tell you that he is, or has that which is comparable to that which you desire to be or have. As you mentally hear and see him, feel the thrill of his good fortune and sincerely wish him well. This awakens in him the corresponding vibration of the state affirmed, which vibration must then objectify itself as a physical fact. You will discover the truth of the statement, "Blessed are the merciful for they shall receive mercy." "The quality of mercy is twice blessed—it blesses him who taketh and him who giveth." The good you subjectively accept as true of others will not only be expressed by them, but a full share will be realized by you.

Transformations are never total. Force A is always transformed into more than a force B. A blow with a hammer produces not only a mechanical concussion, but also heat, electricity, a sound, a magnetic change and so on. The vibratory correlate in the subject is not the entire transformation of the sentiment communicated. The gift transmitted to another is like the divine measure, pressed down, shaken together and running over, so that after the five thousand are fed from the five loaves and two fish, twelve baskets full are left over.

Chapter 7
THE GREATEST PRAYER

Imagination is the beginning of creation. You imagine what you desire, and then you believe it to be true. Every dream could be realized by those self-disciplined enough to believe it. People are what you choose to make them; a man is according to the manner in which you look at him. You must look at him with different eyes before he will objectively change. "Two men looked from the prison bars, one saw the mud and the other saw the stars." Centuries ago, Isaiah asked the question: "Who is blind, but my servant, or deaf, as my messenger that I sent?" "Who is blind as he that is perfect, and blind as the Lord's servant?" The perfect man judges not after appearances, but judges righteously. He sees others as he desires them to be; he hears only what he wants to hear. He sees only the good in others. In him is no condemnation for he transforms the world with his seeing and hearing.

"The king that sitteth on the throne scattereth the evil with his eye." Sympathy for living things—agreement with human limitations—is not in the consciousness of the king because he has learned to separate their false concepts from their true being. To him poverty is but the sleep of wealth. He does not see caterpillars, but painted butterflies to be; not winter, but summer sleeping; not man in want, but Jesus sleeping. Jesus of Nazareth, who scattereth the evil with his eye, is asleep in the imagination of every man, and out of his own imagination must man awaken him by subjectively affirming "I AM

Jesus." Then and only then will he see Jesus, for man can only see what is awake within himself. The holy womb is man's imagination. The holy child is that conception of himself which fits Isaiah's definition of perfection. Heed the words of St. Augustine, "Too late have I loved thee, for behold thou wert within and it was without that I did seek thee." It is to your own consciousness that you must turn as to the only reality. There, and there alone, you awaken that which is asleep. "Though Christ a thousand times in Bethlehem be born, if He is not born in thee thy soul is still forlorn."

Creation is finished. You call your creation into being by feeling the reality of the state you would call. A mood attracts its affinities but it does not create what it attracts. As sleep is called by feeling "I am sleepy," so, too, is Jesus Christ called by the feeling, "I am Jesus Christ." Man sees only himself. Nothing befalls man that is not of the nature of himself. People emerge out of the mass betraying their close affinity to your moods as they are engendered. You meet them seemingly by accident but find they are intimates of your moods. Because your moods continually externalize themselves you could prophesy from your moods, that you, without search, would soon meet certain characters and encounter certain conditions. Therefore call the perfect one into being by living in the feeling, "I am Christ," for Christ is the one concept of self through which can be seen the unveiled realities of eternity.

Our behavior is influenced by our subconscious assumption respecting our own social and intellectual rank and that of the one we are addressing. Let us seek for and evoke the greatest rank, and the noblest of all is that which disrobes man of his mortality and clothes him with uncurbed immortal glory. Let us assume the feeling, "I am Christ," and our whole behavior will subtly and unconsciously change in accordance with that assumption.

Our subconscious assumptions continually externalize themselves that others may consciously see us as we subconsciously see ourselves, and tell us by their actions what we have subconsciously assumed ourselves to be. Therefore let us assume the feeling, "I AM Christ," until our conscious claim becomes our subconscious assumption that "We all with open face beholding as in a glass the glory of the Lord are changed into the same image from glory to glory." Let God awake and His enemies be destroyed. There is no greater prayer for man.

CHAPTER 5

"Remaining Faithful to an Idea"

From *Five Lessons*, 1948

... When I was a boy I lived in a very limited environment, in a little island called Barbados. Feed for animals was very, very scarce and very expensive because we had to import it. I am one of a family of ten children and my grandmother lived with us making thirteen at the table.

Time and again, I can remember my mother saying to the cook in the early part of the week, "I want you to put away three ducks for Sunday's dinner." This meant that she would take from the flock in the yard three ducks and coop them up in a very small cage and feed them, stuff them morning, noon, and night with corn and all the things she wanted the ducks to feast upon.

This was an entirely different diet from what we regularly fed the ducks, because we kept those birds alive by feeding them fish. We kept them alive and fat on fish because fish were very cheap and plentiful; but you could not eat a bird that fed upon fish, not as you and I like a bird.

The cook would take three ducks, put them in a cage and for seven days stuff them with corn, sour milk and all the things we wanted to taste in the birds. Then when they were killed and served for dinner seven days later they were luscious, milk fed, corn fed birds.

But occasionally the cook forgot to put away the birds, and my father, knowing we were having ducks, and believing that she had carried out the command, did not send anything else for dinner, and three fish came to the table. *You could not touch those birds for they were so much the embodiment of what they fed upon.*

Man is a psychological being, a thinker. It is not what he feeds upon physically, but what he feeds upon mentally that he becomes. *We become the embodiment of that which we mentally feed upon.*

Now those ducks could not be fed corn in the morning and fish in the afternoon and something else at night. It had to be a complete change of diet. In our case we cannot have a little bit of meditation in the morning, curse at noon, and do something else in the evening. *We have to go on a mental diet, for a week we must completely change our mental food.*

"Whatsoever things are true, whatsoever things are honest, whatsoever things are just, whatsoever things are pure, whatsoever things are of good report; if there be any virtue, and if there be any praise, think on these things." Philippians 4:8

As a man thinketh in his heart so is he. If I could now single out the kind of mental food I want to express within my world and feast upon it, I would become it.

Let me tell you why I am doing what I am doing today. It was back in 1933 in the city of New York, and my old friend Abdullah, with whom I studied Hebrew for five years, was really the beginning of the eating of all my superstitions. When I went to him I was filled with superstitions. I could not eat meat, I could not eat fish, I could not eat chicken, I could not eat any of these things that were living in the world. I did not drink, I did not smoke, and I was making a tremendous effort to live a celibate life.

Abdullah said to me, "I am not going to tell you 'you are crazy' Neville, but you are you know. All these things are stupid." But I could not believe they were stupid.

In November, 1933, I bade goodbye to my parents in the city of New York as they sailed for Barbados. I had been in this country twelve years with no desire to see Barbados. I was not successful and I was ashamed to go home to successful members of my family. After twelve years in America I was a failure in my own eyes. I was in the theater and made money one year and spent it the next month. I was not what I would call by their standards nor by mine a successful person.

Mind you when I said goodbye to my parents in November I had no desire to go to Barbados. The ship pulled out, and as I came up the street, something possessed me with a desire to go to Barbados.

It was the year 1933, I was unemployed and had no place to go except a little room on 75th Street. I went straight to my old friend Abdullah and said to him "Ab, the strangest feeling is possessing me. For the first time in 12 years I want to go to Barbados."

"If you want to go Neville, you have gone." he replied.

That was very strange language to me. I am in New York City on 72nd Street [at Abdullah's home] and he tells me I have gone to Barbados. I said to him, "What do you mean, I have gone, Abdullah?"

He said, "Do you really want to go?"

I answered, "Yes."

He then said to me, "As you walk through this door now you are not walking on 72nd Street, you are walking on palm-lined streets, coconut-lined streets; this is Barbados. Do not ask me how you are going to go. You are in Barbados. You do not say 'how' when you 'are there'. You are there. Now you walk as though you were there."

I went out of his place in a daze. I am in Barbados. I have no money, I have no job, I am not even well clothed, and yet I am in Barbados.

He was not the kind of a person with whom you would argue, not Abdullah. Two weeks later I was no nearer my goal than on the day I first told him I wanted to go to Barbados. I said to him, "Ab, I trust you implicitly but here is one time I cannot see how it is going to work. I have not one penny towards my journey, I began to explain."

You know what he did. He was as black as the ace of spades, my old friend Abdullah, with his turbaned head. As I sat in his living room he rose from his chair and went towards his study and slammed the door, which was not an invitation to follow him. As he went through the door he said to me, "I have said all that I have to say."

On the 3rd of December I stood before Abdullah and told him again I was no nearer my trip. He repeated his statement, "You are in Barbados."

The very last ship sailing for Barbados that would take me there for the reason I wanted to go, which was to be there for Christmas, sailed at noon on December 6th, the old Nerissa.

On the morning of December 4th, having no job, having no place to go, I slept late. When I got up there was an air mail letter from Barbados under my door. As I opened the letter a little piece of paper flickered to the floor. I picked it up and it was a draft for $50.00.

The letter was from my brother Victor and it read, "I am not asking you to come, Neville, this is a command. We have never had a Christmas when all the members of our family were present at the same time. This Christmas it could be done if you would come."

My oldest brother Cecil left home before the youngest was born and then we started to move away from home at different times so never in the history of our family were we ever all together at the same time.

The letter continued, "You are not working, I know there is no reason why you cannot come, so you must be here before Christmas. The enclosed $50.00 is to buy a few shirts or a pair of shoes you may need for the trip. You will not need tips; use the bar if you are drinking. I will meet the ship and pay all your tips and your incurred expenses. I have cabled Furness, Withy & Co. in New York City and told them to issue you a ticket when you appear at their office. The $50.00 is simply to buy some little essentials. You may sign as you want aboard the ship. I will meet it and take care of all obligations."

I went down to Furness, Withy & Co. with my letter and let them read it. They said, "We received the cable Mr. Goddard, but unfortunately we have not any space left on the December 6th sailing. The only thing available is 3rd Class between New York and St. Thomas. When we get to St. Thomas we have a few passengers who are getting off. You may then ride 1st Class from St. Thomas to Barbados. But between New York and St. Thomas you must go 3rd Class, although you may have the privileges of the First Class dining room and walk the decks of the First Class."

I said, "I will take it."

I went back to my friend Abdullah on the afternoon of December 4th and said, "It worked like a dream." I told him what I had done, thinking he would be happy.

Do you know what he said to me? He said, "Who told you that you are going Third Class? Did I see you in Barbados, the man you are, going Third Class? You are in Barbados and you went there First Class."

I did not have one moment to see him again before I sailed on the noon of December 6th. When I reached the dock with my passport and my papers to get aboard that ship the agent said to me, "We have good news for you, Mr. Goddard. There has been a cancellation and you are going First Class."

Abdullah taught me the importance of remaining faithful to an idea and not compromising. I wavered, but he remained faithful to the assumption that I was in Barbados and had traveled First Class.

CHAPTER 6

"Desire Is the Mainspring of Action"

From *Five Lessons*, 1948

. . . My concept of myself molds a world in harmony with itself and draws men *to tell me constantly by their behavior who I am.*

The most important thing in this world to you is your concept of self. When you dislike your environment, the circumstances of life and the behavior of men, ask yourself, "Who am I?" It is your answer to this question that is the cause of your dislikes.

If you do not condemn self, there will be no man in your world to condemn you. If you are living in the consciousness of your ideal you will see nothing to condemn. "To the pure all things are pure."

Now I would like to spend a little time making as clear as I can what I personally do when I pray, what I do when I want to bring about changes in my world. You will find it interesting, and you will find that it works. No one here can tell me they cannot do it. It is so very simple all can do it. *We are what we imagine we are.*

This technique is not difficult to follow, but you must want to do it. You cannot approach it with the attitude of mind "Oh well, I'll try it." You must want to do it, because the mainspring of action is desire.

Desire is the mainspring of all action. Now what do I want? I must define my objective. For example, suppose I wanted now to be elsewhere. This very moment I really desire to be elsewhere. I need not go through the door, I need not sit down. I need do nothing but stand just where I am and with my eyes closed, *assume that I am actually standing where I desire to be. Then I remain in this state until it has the feeling of reality.* Were I now elsewhere I could not see the world as I now see it from here. The world changes in its relationship to me as I change my position in space.

So I stand right here, close my eyes, and imagine I am seeing what I would see were I there. I remain in it long enough to feel it to be real. I cannot touch the walls of this room from here, but when you close your eyes and become still you can imagine and feel that you touch it. You can stand where you are and imagine you are putting your hand on that wall.

To prove you really are, put it there and slide it up and feel the wood. You can imagine you are doing it without getting off your seat. You can do it and you will actually feel it if you become still enough and intense enough.

I stand where I am and I allow the world that I want to see and to enter physically to come before me as though I were there now. In other words, I bring elsewhere here by assuming that I am there.

Is that clear? I let it come up, I do not make it come up. I simply imagine I am there and then let it happen.

If I want a physical presence, I imagine he is standing here, and I touch him All through the Bible I find these suggestions, "He placed his hands upon them. He touched them."

If you want to comfort someone, what is the automatic feeling? To put your hand on them, you cannot resist it. You meet a friend and the hand goes out automatically, you either shake hands or put your hand on his shoulder.

Suppose you were now to meet a friend that you have not seen for a year and he is a friend of whom you are very fond. What would you do? You would embrace him, wouldn't you? Or you would put your hand upon him.

In your imagination bring him close enough to put your hand upon him and feel him to be solidly real. *Restrict the action to just that.* You will be amazed at what happens. From then on things begin to move. *Your dimensionally greater Self will inspire, in all, the ideas and actions necessary to bring you into physical contact.* It works that way.

Every day I put myself into the drowsy state; it is a very easy thing to do. But habit is a strange thing in man's world. It is not law, but habit acts as though it were the most compelling law in the world. We are creatures of habit.

If you create an interval every day into which you put yourself into the drowsy state, say at 3 o'clock in the afternoon do you know at that moment everyday you will feel drowsy. You try it for one week and see if I am not right.

You sit down for the purpose of creating a state akin to sleep, as though you were sleepy, but do not push the drowsiness too far, just far enough to relax and leave you in control of the direction of your thoughts. You try it for one week, and every day at that hour, no matter what you are doing, you will hardly be able to keep your eyes open. If you know the hour when you will be free you can create it. I would not suggest that you do it lightly, because you will feel very, very sleepy and you may not want to.

I have another way of praying. In this case I always sit down and I find the most comfortable armchair imaginable, or I lie flat on my back and relax completely. Make yourself comfortable. You must not be in any position where the body is distressed. *Always put yourself into a position where you have the greatest ease. That is the first stage.*

To know what you want is the start of prayer. Secondly you construct in your mind's eye one single little event which implies that you have realized your desire. I always let my mind roam on many things that could follow the answered prayer and *I single out one that is most likely to follow the fulfillment of my desire. One simple little thing like the shaking of a hand, embracing a person, the receiving of a letter, the writing of a check, or whatever would imply the fulfillment of your desire.*

After you have decided on the action which implies that your desire has been realized, then sit in your nice comfortable chair or lie flat on your back, *close your eyes for the simple reason it helps to induce this state that borders on sleep.*

The minute you feel this lovely drowsy state, or the feeling of gathered togetherness, wherein you feel, I could move if I wanted to, but I do not want to; I could open my eyes if I wanted to, but I do not want to. *When you get that feeling you can be quite sure that you are in the perfect state to pray successfully.*

In this feeling it is easy to touch anything in this world. You take the simple little restricted action which implies fulfillment of your prayer and you feel it or you enact it. Whatever it is, you enter into the action as though you were an actor in the part. *You do not sit back and visualize yourself doing it. You do it.*

With the body immobilized you imagine that the greater you inside the physical body is coming out of it and that you are actually performing the proposed action. If you are going to walk, you imagine that you are walking. Do not see yourself walk, feel that you are walking.

If you are going to climb stairs, feel that you are climbing the stairs. Do not visualize yourself doing it, feel yourself doing it. If you are going to shake a man's hand, do not visualize yourself shaking his hand, imagine your friend is standing before you and shake his hand. But leave your physical hands immobilized and imagine that your greater hand, which is your imaginary hand, is actually shaking his hand.

All you need do is to imagine that you are doing it. *You are stretched out in time, and what you are doing, which seems to be a controlled daydream, is an actual act in the greater dimension of your being.* You are actually encountering an event fourth-dimensionally before you encounter it here in the three-dimensions of space, and you do not have to raise a finger to bring that state to pass.

My third way of praying is simply to feel thankful. If I want something, either for myself or another, I immobilize the physical body, *then I produce the state akin to sleep and in that state just feel happy, feel thankful, which thankfulness implies realization of what I want. I assume the feeling of the wish fulfilled and with my mind dominated by this single sensation I go to sleep. I need do nothing to make it so, because it is so. My feeling of the wish fulfilled implies it is done.*

All these techniques you can use and change them to fit your temperament. But I must emphasize the necessity of inducing the drowsy state where you can become attentive without effort.

A single sensation dominates the mind, if you pray successfully. What would I feel like, now, were I what I want to be? When I know what the feeling would be like I then close my eyes and lose myself in that single sensation and *my dimensionally greater self then builds a bridge of incident to lead me from this present moment to the fulfillment of my mood. That is all you need do. But people have a habit of slighting the importance of simple things . . .*

CHAPTER 7

"Feed the Mind with Premises"

From *Five Lessons*, 1948

. . . Desire, physical immobility bordering on sleep, and imaginary action in which Self feelingly predominates here and now, are not only important factors in altering the future, but they are also essential conditions in consciously projecting the spiritual Self.

When the physical body is immobilized and we become possessed of the idea to do something—if we imagine that we are doing it here and now and keep the imaginary action feelingly going right up until sleep ensues—we are likely to awaken out of the physical body to find ourselves in a dimensionally larger world with a dimensionally larger focus and actually doing what we desired and imagined we were doing in the flesh.

But whether we awaken there or not, we are actually performing the action in the fourth-dimensional world and will in the future reenact it here in the third-dimensional world. *Experience has taught me to restrict the imaginary action, to condense the idea which is to be the object of our meditation into a single act, and to reenact it over and over again until it has the feeling of reality.* Otherwise, the attention will wander off along an associational track, and hosts of associated images will be presented to our attention, and in a few seconds they will lead us hundreds of miles away from our objective in point of space, and years away in point of time.

If we decide to climb a particular flight of stairs, because that is the likely event to follow the realization of our desire, then we must restrict the action to climbing that particular flight of stairs. *Should the attention wander off, bring it back to its task of climbing that flight of stairs, and keep on doing so until the imaginary action has all the solidity and distinctness of reality. The idea must be maintained in the field of presentation without any sensible effort on our part. We must, with the minimum of effort, permeate the mind with the feeling of the wish fulfilled.*

Drowsiness facilitates change because it favors attention without effort, but it must not be pushed to the state of sleep, in which we shall no longer be able to control the movements of our attention, but a moderate degree of drowsiness in which we are still able to direct our thoughts.

A most effective way to embody a desire is to assume the feeling of the wish fulfilled and then, in a relaxed and sleepy state, repeat over and over again like a lullaby, any short phrase which implies fulfillment of your desire, such as, "Thank you, thank you, thank you," until the single sensation of thankfulness dominates the mind. Speak these words as though you addressed a higher power for having done it for you.

If, however, we seek a conscious projection in a dimensionally larger world, then we must keep the action going right up until sleep ensues. Experience in imagination with all the distinctness of reality what would be experienced in the flesh were we to achieve our goal and we shall in time meet it in the flesh as we met it in our imagination.

Feed the mind with premises—that is, assertions presumed to be true, because assumptions, though false, if persisted in until they have the feeling of reality, will harden into fact.

To an assumption, all means which promote its realization are good. It influences the behavior of all, by inspiring in all the movements, the actions, and the words which tend towards its fulfillment.

To understand how man molds his future in harmony with his assumption—by simply experiencing in his imagination what he would experience in reality were he to realize his goal—we must know what we mean by a dimensionally larger world, for it is to a dimensionally larger world that we go to alter our future.

The observation of an event before it occurs implies that the event is predetermined from the point of view of man in the three-dimensional world. Therefore to change the conditions here in the three dimensions of space we must first change them in the four dimensions of space.

Man does not know exactly what is meant by a dimensionally larger world, and would no doubt deny the existence of a dimensionally larger Self. He is quite familiar with the three dimensions of length, width and height, and he feels that, if there were a fourth dimension, it should be just as obvious to him as the dimensions of length, width and height.

Now a dimension is not a line. It is any way in which a thing can be measured that is entirely different from all other ways. That is, to measure a solid fourth-dimensionally, we simply measure it in any direction except that of its length, width and height.

Now, is there another way of measuring an object other than those of its length, width and height?

Time measures my life without employing the three dimensions of length, width and height. There is no such thing as an instantaneous object. Its appearance and disappearance are measurable. It endures for a definite length of time. We can measure its life span without using the dimensions of length, width and height. Time is definitely a fourth way of measuring an object.

The more dimensions an object has, the more substantial and real it becomes. A straight line, which lies entirely in one dimension, acquires shape, mass and substance by the addition of dimensions. What new quality would time, the fourth dimension give, which would make it just as vastly superior to solids, as solids are to surfaces and surfaces are to lines? *Time is a medium for changes in experience, for all changes take time.*

The new quality is changeability. Observe that, if we bisect a solid, its cross section will be a surface; by bisecting a surface, we obtain a line, and by bisecting a line, we get a point. This means that a point is but a cross section of a line; which is, in turn, but across section of a surface; which is, in turn, but a cross section of a solid; which is, in turn, if carried to its logical conclusion, but across section of a four-dimensional object.

We cannot avoid the inference that all three-dimensional objects are but cross sections of four-dimensional bodies. Which means: when I meet you, I meet a cross section of the four-dimensional you—the four-dimensional Self that is not seen. To see the four-dimensional Self I must see every cross section or moment of your life from birth to death, and see them all as coexisting.

My focus should take in the entire array of sensory impressions which you have experienced on earth, plus those you might encounter. I should see them, not in the order in which they were experienced by you, but as a present whole. *Because change is the characteristic of the fourth dimension, I should see them in a state of flux—as a living, animated whole.*

Now, if we have all this clearly fixed in our minds, what does it mean to us in this three-dimensional world? *It means that, if we can move along times length, we can see the future and alter it if we so desire.*

This world, which we think so solidly real, is a shadow out of which and beyond which we may at any time pass. It is an abstraction from a more fundamental and dimensionally larger world—a more fundamental world abstracted from a still more fundamental and dimensionally larger world—and so on to infinity. For the absolute is unattainable by any means or analysis, no matter how many dimensions we add to the world.

Man can prove the existence of a dimensionally larger world by simply focusing his attention on an invisible state and imagining that he sees and feels it. If he remains concentrated in this state, his present environment will pass away, and he will awaken in a dimensionally larger world where the object of his contemplation will be seen as a concrete objective reality.

I feel intuitively that, were he to abstract his thoughts from this dimensionally larger world and retreat still farther within his mind, he would again bring about an externalization of time. He would discover that, every time he retreats into his inner mind and brings about an externalization of time, space becomes dimensionally larger. And he would therefore conclude that both time and space are serial, and that the drama of life is but the climbing of a multitudinous dimensional time block.

Scientists will one day explain why there is a serial universe. But in practice how we use this serial universe to change the future is more important. To change the future, we need only concern ourselves with two worlds in the infinite series; the world we know by reason of our bodily organs, and the world we perceive independently of our bodily organs.

I have stated that man has at every moment of time the choice before him which of several futures he will have. But the question arises: "How is this possible when the experiences of man, awake in the three-dimensional world, are predetermined?" as his observation of an event before it occurs implies.

This ability to change the future will be seen if we liken the experiences of life on earth to this printed page. Man experiences events on earth singly and successively in the same way that you are now experiencing the words of this page.

Imagine that every word on this page represents a single sensory impression. To get the context, to understand my meaning, you focus your vision on the first word in the upper left-hand corner and then move your focus across the page from left to right, letting it fall on the words singly and successively. By the time your eyes reach the last word on this page you have extracted my meaning.

But suppose on looking at the page, with all the printed words thereon equally present, you decided to rearrange them. You could, by rearranging them, tell an entirely different story, in fact you could tell many different stories.

A dream is nothing more than uncontrolled four-dimensional thinking, or the rearrangement of both past and future sensory impressions. Man seldom dreams of events in the order in which he experiences them when awake. He usually dreams of two or more events which are separated in time fused into a single sensory impression; or else he so completely rearranges his single waking sensory impressions that he does not recognize them when he encounters them in his waking state . . .

. . . *In applying this technique to change the future it is important always to remember that the only thing which occupies the mind during the waking dream is the waking dream, the predetermined action and sensation which implies the fulfillment of our desire.* How the waking dream becomes physical fact is not our concern. Our acceptance of the waking dream as physical reality wills the means for its fulfillment.

Let me again lay the foundation of prayer, which is nothing more than a controlled waking dream:

1. Define your objective, know definitely what you want.

2. *Construct an event which you believe you will encounter following the fulfillment of your desire*—something which will have the action of Self predominant—an event which implies the fulfillment of your desire.

3. *Immobilize the physical body and induce a state of consciousness akin to sleep. Then, mentally feel yourself right into the proposed action, until the single sensation of fulfill-*

ment dominates the mind; imagining all the while that you are actually performing the action here and now so that you experience in imagination what you would experience in the flesh were you now to realize your goal. Experience has convinced me that this is the easiest way to achieve our goal.

However, my own many failures would convict me were I to imply that I have completely mastered the movements of my attention. But I can, with the ancient teacher, say: "This one thing I do, forgetting those things which are behind, and reaching forth unto those things which are before, I press toward the mark for the prize." Philippians 3:13,14 . . .

. . . [Neville's response to question on how to be married:] Forever in love with ideals, it is the ideal state that captures the mind. *Do not confine the state of marriage to a certain man, but a full, rich, and overflowing life. You desire to experience the joy of marriage. Do not modify your dream but enhance it by making it lovelier. Then condense your desire into a single sensation, or act which implies its fulfillment.*

In this western world a woman wears a wedding ring on the third finger of her left hand. Motherhood need not imply marriage; intimacy need not imply marriage, but a wedding ring does.

Relax in a comfortable arm chair, or lie flat on your back and induce a state akin to sleep. Then assume the feeling of being married. Imagine a wedding band on your finger. Touch it. Turn it around the finger. Pull it off over the knuckle. Keep the action going until the ring has the distinctness and feeling of reality. Become so lost in feeling the ring on your finger that when you open your eyes, you will be surprised that it is not there.

If you are a man who does not wear a ring, you could assume greater responsibility. How would you feel if you had a wife to care for? Assume the feeling of being a happily married man right now . . .

CHAPTER 8

"No One to Change But Self"

From *Out of This World*, 1949

*"And for their sakes I sanctify myself, that they
also might be sanctified through the truth."*
—John 17:19.

*The ideal we serve and strive to attain could never
be evolved from us were it not potentially involved
in our nature.*

It is now my purpose to retell and to emphasize
an experience of mine printed by me two years ago.
I believe these quotations from "THE SEARCH"
will help us to understand the operation of the law
of consciousness, and show us that we have no one
to change but self.

Once in an idle interval at sea I meditated on
"the perfect state," and wondered what I would be,
were I of too pure eyes to behold iniquity, if to me

all things were pure and were I without condemnation. As I became lost in this fiery brooding, I found myself lifted above the dark environment of the senses. So intense was feeling I felt myself a being of fire dwelling in a body of air. Voices as from a heavenly chorus, with the exaltation of those who had been conquerors in a conflict with death, were singing, "He is risen—He is risen," and intuitively I knew they meant me.

Then I seemed to be walking in the night. I soon came upon a scene that might have been the ancient Pool of Bethesda for in this place lay a great multitude of impotent folk—blind, halt, withered—waiting not for the moving of the water as of tradition, but waiting for me. As I came near, without thought or effort on my part they were, one after the other, molded as by the Magician of the Beautiful. Eyes, hands, feet—all missing members—were drawn from some invisible reservoir and molded in harmony with that perfection which I felt springing within me. When all were made perfect, the chorus exulted, "It is finished." Then the scene dissolved and I awoke.

I know this vision was the result of my intense meditation upon the idea of perfection, for my meditations invariably bring about union with the state contemplated. I had been so completely absorbed within the idea that for a while I had become what

I contemplated, and the high purpose with which I had for that moment identified myself drew the companionship of high things and fashioned the vision in harmony with my inner nature. The ideal with which we are united works by association of ideas to awaken a thousand moods to create a drama in keeping with the central idea.

My mystical experiences have convinced me that there is no way to bring about the outer perfection we seek other than by the transformation of ourselves. As soon as we succeed in transforming ourselves, the world will melt magically before our eyes and reshape itself in harmony with that which our transformation affirms.

In the divine economy nothing is lost. We cannot lose anything save by descent from the sphere where the thing has its natural life. There is no transforming power in death and, whether we are here or there, we fashion the world that surrounds us by the intensity of our imagination and feeling, and we illuminate or darken our lives by the concepts we hold of ourselves. Noting is more important to us than our conception of ourselves, and especially is this true of our concept of the dimensionally greater One within us.

Those who help or hinder us, whether they know it or not, are the servants of that law which shapes outward circumstances in harmony with our inner nature. It is our conception of ourselves which frees or constrains us, though it may use material agencies to achieve its purpose.

Because life molds the outer world to reflect the inner arrangement of our minds, there is no way of bringing about the outer perfection we seek other than by the transformation of ourselves. No help cometh from without; the hills to which we lift our eyes are those of an inner range. It is thus to our own consciousness that we must turn as to the only reality, the only foundation on which all phenomena can be explained. We can rely absolutely on the justice of this law to give us only that which is of the nature of ourselves.

To attempt to change the world before we change our concept of ourselves is to struggle against the nature of things. There can be no outer change until there is first an inner change. As within, so without. I am not advocating philosophical indifference when I suggest that we should imagine ourselves as already that which we want to be, living in a mental atmosphere of greatness, rather than using physical means and arguments to bring about the desired change. Everything we do, unaccompanied by a change of consciousness, is but futile readjustment of surfaces. However we toil or struggle, we can receive no more than our assumptions affirm. To protest against anything which happens to us is to protest against the law of our being and our rulership over our own destiny.

The circumstances of my life are too closely related to my conception of myself not to have been formed by my own spirit from some dimensionally larger storehouse of my being. If there is pain to me in these happenings, I should look within myself for the cause, for I am moved here and there and made to live in a world in harmony with my concept of myself.

Intense meditation brings about a union with the state contemplated, and during this union we see visions, have experiences and behave in keeping with our change of consciousness. This shows us that a transformation of consciousness will result in a change of environment and behavior.

All wars prove that violent emotions are extremely potent in precipitating mental rearrangements. Every great conflict has been followed by an era of materialism and greed in which the ideals for which the conflict ostensibly was waged are submerged. This is inevitable because war evokes hate which impels a descent in consciousness from the plane of the ideal to the level where the conflict is waged. If we would become as emotionally aroused over our ideals as we become over our dislikes, we would ascend to the plane of our ideal as easily as we now descend to the level of our hates.

Love and hate have a magical transforming power, and we grow through their exercise into the likeness of what we contemplate. By intensity of hatred we create in ourselves the character we imagine in our enemies. Qualities die for want of attention, so the unlovely states might best be rubbed out by imagining "beauty for ashes and joy for mourning" rather than by direct attacks on the state from which we would be free. "Whatsoever things are lovely and of good report, think on these things," for we become that with which we are en rapport.

There is nothing to change but our concept of self. As soon as we succeed in transforming self, our world will dissolve and reshape itself in harmony with that which our change affirms.

CHAPTER 9

"Law of Assumption"

The great mystic, William Blake, wrote almost two hundred years ago, "What seems to be, is, to those to whom it seems to be and is productive of the most dreadful consequences to those to whom it seems to be."

Now, at first, this mystical gem seems a bit involved, or at best to be a play on words; but it is nothing of the kind. Listen to it carefully. "What seems to be, is, to those to whom it seems to be." That is certainly clear enough. It is a simple truth about *the law of assumption*, and a warning of the consequences of its misuse.

The author of the Epistle to the Romans declared in the fourteenth chapter, "I know, and am persuaded by the Lord Jesus, that there is nothing unclean of itself; but to him that esteemeth anything to be unclean, to him it is unclean."

We see by this that it is not superior insight but pure blindness that reads into the greatness of men some littleness with which it chances to be familiar, for what seems to be, is, to those to whom it seems to be.

Experiments recently conducted at two of our leading universities revealed this great truth about the law of assumption. They stated in their releases to the newspapers that after two thousand experiments they came to the conclusion that, "What you see when you look at something depends not so much on what is there as on the assumption you make when you look. What you believe to be the real physical world is actually only an assumptive world."

In other words, you would not define your husband in the same way that your mother would. Yet, you are both defining the same person. Your particular relationship to a thing influences your feelings with respect to that thing and makes you see in it an element which is not there. If your feeling in the matter is a self-element, it can be cast out. If it is a permanent distinction in the state considered, it cannot be cast out. *The thing to do is to try. If you can change your opinion of another, then what you now believe of him cannot be absolutely true, but relatively true.*

Men believe in the reality of the external world because they do not know how to focus and condense their powers to penetrate its thin crust. Strangely enough, it is not difficult to penetrate this view of the senses. To remove the veil of the senses, we do not employ great effort; the objective world vanishes as we turn our attention from it. We have only to concentrate on the state desired to mentally see it; but to give reality to it so that it will become an objective fact, we must focus our attention upon the desired state until it has all the sensory vividness and feeling of reality.

When, through concentrated attention, our desire appears to possess the distinctness and feeling of reality; when the form of thought is as vivid as the form of nature, we have given it the right to become a visible fact in our lives. *Each man must find the means best suited to his nature to control his attention and concentrate it on the desired state.* I find for myself the best state to be one of meditation, a relaxed state akin to sleep, but a state in which I am still consciously in control of my imagination and capable of fixing my attention on a mental object.

If it is difficult to control the direction of your attention while in this state akin to sleep, you may find gazing fixedly into an object very helpful. Do not look at its surface, but rather into and beyond any plain object such as a wall, a carpet or any object which possesses depth. Arrange it to return as little reflection as possible. Imagine, then, that in this depth you are seeing and hearing what you want to see and hear until your attention is exclusively occupied by the imagined state.

At the end of your meditation, when you awake from your controlled waking dream you feel as though you had returned from a great distance. *The visible world which you had shut out returns to consciousness and, by its very presence, informs you that you have been self-deceived into believing that the object of your contemplation was real; but if you remain faithful to your vision this sustained mental attitude will give reality to your visions and they will become visible concrete facts in your world.*

Define your highest ideal and concentrate your attention upon this ideal until you identify yourself with it. Assume the feeling of being it—the feeling that would be yours were you now embodying it in your world. This assumption, though now denied by your senses, *if persisted in*, will become a fact in your world.

You will know when you have succeeded in fixing the desired state in consciousness simply by looking mentally at the people you know. This is a wonderful check on yourself as your mental conversations are more revealing than your physical conversations are. If, in your mental conversations with others, you talk with them as you formerly did, then you have not changed your concept of self, for all changes of concepts of self result in a changed relationship to the world.

Remember what was said earlier, "What you see when you look at something depends not so much on what is there as on the assumption you make when you look." Therefore, the assumption of the wish fulfilled should make you see the world mentally as you would physically were your assumption a physical fact. *The spiritual man speaks to the natural man through the language of desire. The key to progress in life and to the fulfillment of dreams lies in the ready obedience to the voice. Unhesitating obedience to its voice is an immediate assumption of the wish fulfilled. To desire a state is to have it.*

As Pascal said, "You would not have sought me had you not already found me." Man, by assuming the feeling of the wish fulfilled and then living and acting on this conviction changes his future in harmony with his assumption. To "change his future" is the inalienable right of freedom loving individuals. There would be no progress in the world were it not for the divine discontent in man which urges him on to higher and higher levels of consciousness . . .

. . . Since the right to change our future is our birthright as sons of God, let us accept its challenge and learn just how to do it. Again today, speaking of changing your future, I wish to stress the importance of a real transformation of self—not merely a slight alteration of circumstances which, in a matter of moments, will permit us to slip back into the old dissatisfied man. In your meditation, allow others to see you as they would see you were this new concept of self a concrete fact. You always seem to others the embodiment of the ideal you inspire. Therefore, in meditation, when you contemplate others, you must be seen by them mentally as you would be seen by them physically were your conception of yourself an objective fact. That is, in meditation, you imagine that they see you expressing this nobler man you desire to be. If you assume that you are what you want to be, your desire is fulfilled and, in fulfillment, all longing "to be" is neutralized. This, also, is an excellent check on yourself as to whether or not you have actually succeeded in changing self. *You cannot continue desiring what has been realized. Rather, you are in a mood to give thanks for a gift received.* Your desire is not something you labor to fulfill, it is recognizing something you already possess. It is assuming the feeling of being that which you desire to be.

Believing and being are one. The conceiver and his conception are one. Therefore, that which you conceive yourself to be can never be so far off as even to be near, for nearness implies separation. "If thou canst believe, all things are possible to him that believeth."

"Faith is the substance of things hoped for, the evidence of things not yet seen." If you assume that you are that finer, nobler one you wish to be, you will see others as they are related to your high assumption.

All enlightened men wish for the good of others. If it is the good of another you seek, you must use the same controlled contemplation. In meditation, you must represent the other to yourself as already being or having the greatness you desire for him. As for yourself, your desire for another must be an intense one. It is through desire that you rise above your present sphere and the road from longing to fulfillment is shortened as you experience in imagination all that you would experience in the flesh were you or your friend the embodiment of the desire you have for yourself or him.

Experience has taught me that this is the perfect way to achieve my great goals for others as well as for myself. However, my own failures would convict me were I to imply that I have completely mastered the control of my attention. I can, however, with the ancient teacher say: "This one thing I do, forgetting those things which are behind, and reaching forth unto those things which are before—I press towards the mark for the prize."

CHAPTER 10

"Failure"

From *The Power of the Awareness*, 1952

This book would not be complete without some discussion of failure in the attempted use of the law of assumption. It is entirely possible that you either have had or will have a number of failures in this respect—many of them in really important matters. If, having read this book, having a thorough knowledge of the application and working of the law of assumption, you faithfully apply it in an effort to attain some intense desire and fail, what is the reason? If to the question, did you persist enough?, you can answer yes—and still the attainment of your desire was not realized, what is the reason for failure?

The answer to this is the most important factor in the successful use of the law of assumption. *The time it takes your assumption to become fact, your desire to be fulfilled, is directly proportionate to the naturalness of your feeling of already being what you want to be—of already having what you desire.*

The fact that it does not feel natural to you to be what you imagine yourself to be is the secret of your failure. Regardless of your desire, regardless of how faithfully and intelligently you follow the law if you do not feel natural about what you want to be *you will not be it.* If it does not feel natural to you to get a better job you will not get a better job. The whole principle is vividly expressed by the Bible phrase "you die in your sins"—you do not transcend from your present level to the state desired. How can this feeling of naturalness be achieved? The secret lies in one word—*imagination.* For example, this is a very simple illustration. Assume that you are securely chained to a large heavy iron bench. You could not possibly run, in fact you could not even walk. In these circumstances it would not be natural for you to run. You could not even *feel* that it was natural for you to run. But you could easily *imagine* yourself running. In that instant, while your consciousness is filled with your *imagined* running, you have forgotten that you are bound. In *imagination* your running was completely natural.

The essential feeling of naturalness can be achieved by *persistently filling your consciousness with imagination*—imagining yourself being what you want to be or having what you desire.

Progress can spring only from your imagination, from your desire to transcend your present level. What you truly and literally must feel is that *with your imagination, all things are possible*. You must realize that changes are not caused by caprice, but by a change of consciousness. You may fail to achieve or sustain the particular state of consciousness necessary to produce the effect you desire. But, once you know that consciousness is the only reality and is the sole creator of your particular world and have burnt this truth into your whole being, then you know that success or failure is entirely in your own hands. Whether or not you are disciplined enough to sustain the required state of consciousness in specific instances has no bearing on the truth of the law itself—that an assumption, if persisted in, will harden into fact. The certainty of the truth of this law must remain despite great disappointment and tragedy—even when you "see the light of life go out and all the world go on as though it were still day." You must not believe that because your assumption failed to materialize, the truth that assumptions do materialize is a lie. *If your assumptions are not fulfilled it is because of some error or weakness in your consciousness. However, these errors and weaknesses can be overcome. Therefore, press on to the attainment of ever higher levels by feeling that you already are the person you want to be. And remember that the time it takes your assumption to become reality is proportionate to the naturalness of being it.*

Man surrounds himself with the true image of himself. Every spirit builds itself a house and beyond its house a world, and beyond its world a heaven. Know then that the world exists for you. For you the phenomenon is perfect. What we are, that only can we see. All that Adam had, all that Caesar could, you have and can do. Adam called his house, heaven and earth. Caesar called his house, Rome; you perhaps call yours a cobbler's trade; a hundred acres of land, or a scholar's garret. Yet line for line and point for point, your dominion is as great as theirs, though without fine name. Build therefore your own world. As fast as you conform your life to the pure idea in your mind, that will unfold its great proportion.

—EMERSON

CHAPTER 11

"Prayer Is a Surrender"

———————

Radio lecture, KECA,
Los Angeles, July 1953

Have you ever had a prayer answered? What wouldn't men give just to feel certain that when they pray, something definite would happen. For this reason, I would like to take a little time to see why it is that some prayers are answered and some apparently fall on dry ground.

"When ye pray, believe that ye receive, and ye shall receive." Believe that ye receive—is the condition imposed upon man. Unless we believe that we receive, our prayer will not be answered. A prayer—granted—implies that something is done in consequence of the prayer which otherwise would not have been done. Therefore, the one who prays is the spring of action—the directing mind—and the one who grants the prayer. Such responsibility man refuses to assume, for responsibility, it seems, is mankind's invisible nightmare.

The whole natural world is built on law. Yet, between prayer and its answer we see no such relation. We feel that God may answer or ignore our prayer, that our prayer may hit the mark or may miss it. The mind is still unwilling to admit that God subjects Himself to His own laws. How many people believe that there is, between prayer and its answer, a relation of cause and effect?

Let us take a look at the means employed to heal the ten lepers as related in the seventeenth chapter of the Gospel of St. Luke. The thing that strikes us in this story is the method that was used to raise their faith to the needful intensity. We are told that the ten lepers appealed to Jesus to "have mercy" on them, that is to heal them. Jesus ordered them to go and show themselves to the priests, and "as they went, they were cleansed."

The Mosaic Law demanded that when a leper recovered from his disease he must show himself to the priest to obtain a certificate of restored health. Jesus imposed a test upon the lepers' faith and supplied a means by which their faith could be raised to its full potency. If the lepers refused to go—they had no faith—and, therefore, could not be healed. But, if they obeyed Him, the full realization of what their journey implied would break upon their minds as they went and this dynamic thought would heal them. So, we read, "As they went, they were cleansed."

You, no doubt, often have heard the words of that inspiring old hymn—"Oh, what peace we often forfeit; oh, what needless pain we bear, all because we do not carry everything to God in prayer." I, myself, came to this conviction through experience, being led to brood upon the nature of prayer. I believe in the practice and philosophy of what men call prayer, but not everything that receives that name is really prayer.

Prayer is the elevation of the mind to that which we seek. The very first word of correction is always "arise." Always lift the mind to that which we seek. This is easily done by assuming the feeling of the wish fulfilled. How would you feel if your prayer were answered? Well, assume that feeling until you experience in imagination what you would experience in reality if your prayer were answered. *Prayer means getting into action mentally.* It means holding the attention upon the idea of the wish fulfilled until it fills the mind and crowds all other ideas out of the consciousness.

This statement that prayer means getting into action mentally and holding the attention upon the idea of the wish fulfilled until it fills the mind and crowds all other ideas out of the consciousness, does not mean that prayer is a mental effort—an act of will. On the contrary, prayer is to be contrasted with an act of will. *Prayer is a surrender.* It means abandoning oneself to the feeling of the wish fulfilled. If prayer brings no response, there is something wrong with the prayer and the fault lies generally in *too much effort.* Serious confusion arises insofar as men identify the state of prayer with an act of will, instead of contrasting it with an act of will. *The sovereign rule is to make no effort, and if this is observed, you will intuitively fall into the right attitude.*

Creativeness is not an act of will, but a deeper receptiveness—a keener susceptibility. The acceptance of the end—the acceptance of the answered prayer—finds the means for its realization. Feel yourself into the state of the answered prayer until the state fills the mind and crowds all other states out of your consciousness. *What we must work for is not the development of the will, but the education of the imagination and the steadying of attention.* Prayer succeeds by avoiding conflict. Prayer is, above all things, easy. Its greatest enemy is effort. The mighty surrenders itself fully only to that which is most gentle. The wealth of Heaven may not be seized by a strong will, but surrenders itself, a free gift, to the God-spent moment. Along the lines of least resistance travel spiritual as well as physical forces.

We must act on the assumption that we already possess that which we desire, for all that we desire is already present within us. It only waits to be claimed. That it must be claimed is a necessary condition by which we realize our desires. Our prayers are answered if we assume the feeling of the wish fulfilled and continue in that assumption.

One of the loveliest examples of an answered prayer I witnessed in my own living room. A very charming lady from out of town came to see me concerning prayer. As she had no one with whom to leave her eight-year old son, she brought him with her the time of our interview. Seemingly, he was engrossed in playing with a toy truck, but at the end of the interview with his mother he said, "Mr. Neville, I know how to pray now. I know what I want—a collie puppy—and I can imagine I am hugging him every night on my bed."

His mother explained to him and to me the impossibilities of his prayer, the cost of the puppy, their confined home, even his inability to care for the dog properly. The boy looked into his mother's eyes and simply said, "But, Mother, I know how to pray now."

And he did. Two months later during a "Kindness to Animals Week" in his city, all the school children were required to write an essay on how they would love and care for a pet. You have guessed the answer. His essay, out of the five thousand submitted, won the prize, and that prize, presented by the mayor of the city to the lad was a collie puppy. The boy truly assumed the feeling of his wish fulfilled, *hugging and loving his puppy every night . . .*

. . . Prayer is a controlled waking dream. *If we are to pray successfully, we must steady our attention to observe the world as it would be seen by us were our prayer answered.*

Steadying attention makes no call upon any special faculty, but it does demand control of imagination. We must extend our senses—observe our changed relationship to our world and trust this observation.

The new world is not there to grasp, but to sense, to touch. The best way to observe it is to be intensely aware of it. In other words, we can, by listening as though we heard and by looking as though we saw, actually hear voices and see scenes from within ourselves that are otherwise not audible or visible. With our attention focused on the state desired, the outer world crumbles and then the world—like music—by a new setting, turns all its discords into harmonies.

Life is not a struggle but a surrender. Our prayers are answered by the powers we invoke *not by those we exert.*

So long as the eyes take notice, the soul is blind—for the world that moves us is the one we imagine, not the world round about us. *We must yield our whole being to the feeling of being the noble one we want to be*. If anything is kept back, the prayer is vain. We often are deprived of our high goal by our effort to possess it. *We are called upon to act on the assumption that we already are the man we would be.* If we do this without effort—experiencing in imagination what we would experience in the flesh had we realized our goal, we shall find that we do, indeed, possess it. The healing touch is in our attitude. We need change nothing but our attitude towards it. Assume a virtue if you have it not, assume the feeling of your wish fulfilled. "Pray for my soul; more things are wrought by prayer than this world dreams of."

CHAPTER 12

"Sound Investments"

Lecture, 1953

I want to share with you today what I consider one of the truly great revelations of all time.

On Sunday morning, April 12th, my wife woke from what was really a deep, profound sleep and as she was waking a voice distinctly spoke to her. And the voice spoke to her, and the voice spoke with great authority and it said to her: *You must stop spending your thoughts, your time and your money; everything in life must be an investment.*

So she quickly wrote it down and went straight to the dictionary to look up the two important words in the sentence, "spending" and "investing." The dictionary defines "spending" as "to waste, to squander, to layout without return." To "invest" is to "layout for a purpose, for which a profit is expected."

Then I began to analyze the sentence... "You must stop spending your thoughts, your time and your money, for everything in life must be an investment." As I dwelt upon it, I saw where everything is *now*; that through the portals of the present all time must pass, and this psychological *now*, the state in which I find myself now, does not recede into the past. It advances into my future.

So, what I do *now* is the all-important thing, and thought is the coin of heaven; it is the money of heaven; and so the thought I entertain now, the thought to which I consent, as told us in Ephesians "All things when they are admitted are made manifest by the light, and all things when they are manifested are light:" and the word 'light' is defined as consciousness. So the state to which I now consent must be made manifest, and when it is manifest, it is only that state of consciousness made visible, coming to bear witness of the state in which I abided.

So, every moment of time, I am either spending or I am investing. Unfortunately most of us spend the coin of heaven, and morning, noon and night we live in negative states for which there is no return, when we could easily have spent, not spent, but invested that moment, so at the end of that day we really would have a wonderful portfolio.

The religious-minded person invests possibly on Sunday morning. Through the service he is lifted for a moment; if he is not overly critical he might be carried away with the hymn; he might be carried away with the solo, the organ music, the address from the pulpit, and for a moment he is investing; but the rest of the week he spends.

Now you know from experience if you put all your money into one great concern, it may be wonderful, it may be sound, but at the end of a year the directors may decide to reorganize and therefore decide to pass the dividend, and if you depended on a dividend check for your daily needs, though it is a good, firm, wonderful concern, when they passed the dividend, then you must either sell some stock or raise or borrow on it.

While every moment of time you could have a most marvelous portfolio and if one passes a dividend check it does not matter. *If you devoted every moment of time to positive thinking, constructive thinking, by not accepting any rumor that does not contribute to the fulfillment of your desire, no matter what it is—it could be the most obvious fact in the world—if it does not contribute to the fulfillment of your dreams, do not accept it.* If you do you are spending; if, not by denying, but by complete indifference, complete non-acceptance, you turn to what you wish you could have heard instead of what you heard, you are investing. It's not the hearing that matters, it's the admitting the truth of it that matters.

All things when they are admitted, not all things when they are heard, but if you give consent to it, if you accept it as true; then you either spend by acceptance or you invest depending on the nature of the state accepted. So, this revelation which came through my wife to me is one of the greatest that I have heard ... It came in a normal natural manner to instruct not only her, but to instruct her husband, for I was the first one to whom she told it and I can't tell you what it has done to me since I heard it on the morning of the 12th April, for it made me more aware of the moment, made me far more conscious of every moment of the day so that I am not spending; I must invest—time is too precious and because these moments do not recede, they do not pass away; they are always advancing into my future to either confront me with a waste or to show me some wonderful return; if I invest it's for a purpose and, therefore, I hope, not only hope, I expect a reward: I expect a profit on my investment. So a moment spent now, this very day, could tomorrow pay you great dividends ...

... Now we are told in the thirtieth chapter of the Book of Deuteronomy, "The commandment I command you this day is not hidden, and it isn't far off. It's near unto thee; it is in thy mouth and in thy heart. Now, I set before you this day, life and good, death and evil, blessings and cursings. Choose life, choose blessing." But the choice is ours for we are free. He sets before us this day, this very moment, a commandment. He sets everything before us; it's not far away, it's in our tongue right now. And before me now is a blessing or a curse; I can accept the fact you don't like me; it doesn't matter, you may love me; but if I accept the fact that you don't like me, don't like the teaching, I'm spending my time. *Tomorrow you'll prove to me that I have spent my time by your behavior relative to me.* On the other hand, if I accept the fact that you do like it, because you are proving it, then I would have no doubt in my mind that you could not do anything other than contribute to this teaching. *So it is up to me to either bless myself or curse myself.*

I can choose life or I can choose death. I can choose the good, but I am free, I can choose the evil. It's entirely up to me. But if you and I loved this, accept it and believe it, then we are wise indeed if, knowing the whole is before us, we go out determined to become investors, not spenders, not wasting and squandering our substance, but laying it out for a purpose. Every moment become conscious of the moment, what are you doing. I am accepting now the fact that I am a noble, dignified, wonderful being, that my father is proud of the son who is like him. So I will not hear or accept as true anything other than that which contributes to that noble concept I will hold of myself.

For I will see that I am secure, and maybe a headline would startle the world but I will not accept it, for if I don't admit to it, it can't proceed out of me. For all things when they are admitted are made manifest, not unless they are admitted ...

... *All you need is time and you have it, it's now. All you need is the thought, that's money.* So instead of spending that now, and spending the thought in the now, invest it now, for your now, this very moment as I stand here and I will get off the platform in a little while—and you will think, well now this is gone, he'll come back next year—this is not gone. What I am doing now is not going to slip away; it's going to move forward and embody itself as a condition, embody itself as the circumstance of my life. So that my now's, my reactions to what I am hearing and saying and seeing, all of my reactions are in the now, and my reactions are spelling out my tomorrow ... *Every moment of your life see that it is a positive, constructive, noble moment. I promise you a wonderful, healthy, radiant future if you will invest the now ...*

... So here, look out at your world, formulate your lovely aims in life and just ask yourself, "What would it be like were it true that I now embody that state? How would I feel?" And in response to that question would come a feeling, a feeling that corresponds to that end. Learn then to think from that end, though reason denies it, though everything denies it, you occupy that end. It's now, you're investing it and these will become real within your world . . .

. . . And now at the end of the silence, this is what we do. Knowing that any time that we exercise our imagination lovingly on behalf of another, we are actually and literally mediating God to man. So we can sit quietly in the darkness and simply listen as though we heard the good report that we want to hear. We look into the darkness and imagine we are seeing what we want to see. This is then investing this two minutes; we have taken the moments that go to make up two minutes and really are investing it now. So when I take the chair and the lights are lowered let us listen and let us look as though we are hearing and seeing what we want to hear and see. And we are actually fulfilling the command of that wonderful voice that spoke to my wife when it said to her, "You must stop spending your time, your thought, and your money. For everything in life must be an investment." *Let these two minutes be your greatest investment.*

CHAPTER 13

"The Pruning Shears of Revision"

From *Awakened Imagination*, 1954

The very first act of correction or cure is always "revise." One must start with oneself. It is one's attitude that must be changed.

> *"What we are, that only can we see."*
> —Emerson

It is a most healthy and productive exercise to daily relive the day as you wish you had lived it, revising the scenes to make them conform to your ideals. For instance, suppose today's mail brought disappointing news. Revise the letter. Mentally rewrite it and make it conform to the news you wish you had received. Then, in imagination, read the revised letter over and over again. *This is the essence of revision and revision results in repeal.*

The one requisite is to arouse your attention in a way and to such intensity that you become wholly absorbed in the revised action. You will experience an expansion and refinement of the senses by this imaginative exercise and eventually achieve vision. But always remember that the ultimate purpose of this exercise is to create in you "the Spirit of Jesus" which is continual forgiveness of sin.

Revision is of greatest importance when the motive is to change oneself, when there is a sincere desire to be something different, when the longing is to awaken the ideal active spirit of forgiveness. Without imagination man remains a being of sin. Man either goes forward to imagination or remains imprisoned in his senses. To go forward to imagination is to forgive. *Forgiveness is the life of the imagination. The art of living is the art of forgiving. Forgiveness is, in fact, experiencing in imagination the revised version of the day, experiencing in imagination what you wish you had experienced in the flesh. Every time one really forgives; that is, every time one relives the event as it should have been lived, one is born again.*

"Father forgive them" is not the plea that comes once a year but the opportunity that comes every day. The idea of forgiving is a daily possibility, and, if it is sincerely done, it will lift man to higher and higher levels of being. He will experience a daily Easter and Easter is the idea of rising transformed. And that should be almost a continuous process.

Freedom and forgiveness are indissolubly linked. Not to forgive is to be at war with ourselves for we are freed according to our capacity to forgive . . .

. . . You must take pleasure in revision. *You can forgive others effectively only when you have a sincere desire to identify them with their ideal. Duty has no momentum.* Forgiveness is a matter of deliberately withdrawing attention from the unrevised day and giving it full strength and joyously to the revised day. If a man begins to revise even a little of the vexations and troubles of the day, then he begins to work practically on himself. *Every revision is a victory over himself and therefore a victory over his enemy.*

> *"A man's foes are those of his own household."*
> —Matthew 10:36

And his household is his state of mind. He changes his future as he revises his day.

When man practices the art of forgiveness, of revision, however factual the scene on which sight then rests, he revises it with his imagination and gazes on one never before witnessed. The magnitude of the change which any act of revision involves makes such change appear wholly improbable to the realist—the unimaginative man; but the radical changes in the fortunes of the Prodigal were all produced by a "change of heart."

The battle man fights is fought out *in his own imagination*. The man who does not revise the day has lost the vision of that life, into the likeness of which, it is the true labor of the "Spirit of Jesus" to transform this life.

"All things whatsoever ye would that men should do to you, even so do ye to them: for this is the law."
—Matthew 7:12

Here is the way an artist friend forgave herself and was set free from pain, annoyance and unfriendliness. Knowing that nothing but forgetfulness and forgiveness will bring us to new values, she cast herself upon her imagination and escaped from the prison of her senses. She writes:

"Thursday I taught all day in the art school. Only one small thing marred the day. Coming into my afternoon classroom I discovered the janitor had left all the chairs on top of the desks after cleaning the floor. As I lifted a chair down it slipped from my grasp and struck me a sharp blow on the instep of my right foot. I immediately examined my thoughts and found that I had criticized the man for not doing his job properly. Since he had lost his helper I real-ized he probably felt he had done more than enough and it was an unwanted gift that had bounced and hit me on the foot. Looking down at my foot I saw both my skin and nylons were intact so forgot the whole thing.

"That night, after I had been working intensely for about three hours on a drawing, I decided to make myself a cup of coffee. To my utter amazement I couldn't manage my right foot at all and it was giv-ing out great bumps of pain. I hopped over to a chair and took off my slipper to look at it. The entire foot was a strange purplish pink, swollen out of shape and red hot. I tried walking on it and found that it just flapped. I had no control over it whatsoever. It looked like one of two things: either I had cracked a bone when I dropped the chair on it or something could be dislocated.

"'No use speculating what it is. Better get rid of it right away.' So I became quiet all ready to melt myself into light. To my complete bewilderment my imagination refused to cooperate. It just said 'No.' This sort of thing often happens when I am painting. I just started to argue 'Why not?' It just kept saying 'No.' Finally I gave up and said 'You know I am in pain. I am trying hard not to be frightened, but you are the boss. What do you want to do?' The answer: 'Go to bed and review the day's events.' So I said 'All right. But let me tell you if my foot isn't perfect by tomorrow morning you have only yourself to blame.'

"After arranging the bed clothes so they didn't touch my foot I started to review the day. It was slow going as I had difficulty keeping my attention away from my foot. I went through the whole day, saw nothing to add to the chair incident. But when I reached the early evening I found myself coming face to face with a man who for the past year has made a point of not speaking. The first time this happened I thought he had grown deaf. I had known him since school days, but we had never done more than say 'hello' and comment on the weather. Mutual friends assured me I had done nothing, that he had said he never liked me and finally decided it was not worthwhile speaking. I had said 'Hi!' He hadn't answered. I found that I thought 'Poor guy—what a horrid state to be in. I shall do something about this ridiculous state of affairs,' So, in my imagination, I stopped right there and re-did the scene. I said 'Hi!' He answered 'Hi!' and smiled. I now thought 'Good old Ed.' I ran the scene over a couple of times and went on to the next incident and finished up the day.

"'Now what—do we do my foot or the concert?' I had been melting and wrapping up a wonderful present of courage and success for a friend who was to make her debut the following day and I had been looking forward to giving it to her tonight. My imagination sounded a little bit solemn as it said 'Let us do the concert. It will be more fun.' 'But first couldn't we just take my perfectly good imagination foot out of this physical one before we start?' I pleaded. 'By all means.'

"That done, I had a lovely time at the concert and my friend got a tremendous ovation.

"By now I was very, very sleepy and fell asleep doing my project. The next morning, as I was putting on my slipper, I suddenly had a quick memory picture of withdrawing a discolored and swollen foot from the same slipper. I took my foot out and looked at it. It was perfectly normal in every respect. There was a tiny pink spot on the instep where I remembered I had hit it with the chair. 'What a vivid dream that was!' I thought and dressed. While waiting for my coffee I wandered over to my drafting table and saw that all my brushes were lying helter-skelter and unwashed. 'Whatever possessed you to leave your brushes like that?' 'Don't you remember? It was because of your foot.' So it hadn't been a dream after all but a beautiful healing."

She had won by the art of revision what she would never have won by force.

"In Heaven the only Art of Living Is Forgetting &
Forgiving Especially to the Female."
—Blake

We should take our life, not as it appears to be, but from the vision of this artist, from the vision of the world made perfect that is buried under all minds—buried and waiting for us to revise the day.

"We are led to believe a lie when we see with,
not through the eye."
—Blake

A revision of the day, and what she held to be so stubbornly real was no longer so to her and, like a dream, had quietly faded away.

You can revise the day to please yourself and by experiencing in imagination the revised speech and actions not only modify the trend of your life story but turn all its discords into harmonies. The one who discovers the secret of revision cannot do otherwise than let himself be guided by love. Your effectiveness will increase with practice. Revision is the way by which right can find its appropriate might. "Resist not evil" for all passionate conflicts result in an interchange of characteristics.

"To him that knoweth to do good,
and doeth it not, to him it is sin."
—James 4:17

To know the truth you must live the truth and to live the truth your inner actions must match the actions of your fulfilled desire. Expectancy and desire must become one. Your outer world is only actualized inner movement. Through ignorance of the law of revision those who take to warfare are perpetually defeated.

Only concepts that idealize depict the truth.

Your ideal of man is his truest self. It is because I firmly believe that whatever is most profoundly imaginative is, in reality, most directly practical that I ask you to live imaginatively and to think into and to personally appropriate the transcendent saying "Christ in you, the hope of glory."

Don't blame; only resolve. It is not man and the earth at their loveliest, but you practicing the art of revision make paradise. The evidence of this truth can lie only in your own experience of it. Try revising the day. It is to the pruning shears of revision that we owe our prime fruit.

CHAPTER 14

"All Things Are Possible to the Inner Man"

Television talk, KTTV,
Los Angeles, CA, 1955

... If an action is needed you must turn to the inner man and the inner man must do it ... A blind girl was in my audience [in San Francisco]. And she was faced with a problem. Although blind she was earning a wonderful, wonderful income. But there recently came the rerouting of the buses and she found herself spending two-and-a-half hours one way on three buses. For being blind, I tell you now, when I say blind, her eyes are removed; there are little plastic eyes when you look into her eyes—they had to remove them years and years ago.

So, in her predicament, getting off one bus she must wait and hope that someone is passing by and, seeing her limitations, can help her across the street. So she crossed herself and after two weeks she could not make it in less than two-and-a-half hours. And in previous days when she had only one bus to take she made it in fifteen minutes. So, that night this is what she did. She sat in her living room and she first of all investigated what it would cost by taxi. That was completely out of the question. She thought in terms of giving up her apartment. But all the things that she thought of rapidly, she couldn't put into effect. She came to the conclusion that going from her place to the place she worked in a car was the only solution. She couldn't afford a chauffeur and she couldn't drive, for she was blind. But a car seemed to her the only solution.

So this is what she did. Sitting in her living room in a nice easy chair, she assumed that she was seated on the front seat of a car. She felt that the person next to her was a man. Then she felt the rhythm of the car. Then she could smell the gasoline. Then she felt the car move. She felt it stop for what she thought would be a red light. Then she felt the car move on. She finally came to the end of her imaginary journey, she turned to her companion and said, "Thank you very much, sir." To which he replied, "The pleasure is all mine." She got out of that car and then she imagined she heard the door click, as she slammed in her imagination the door of the car. And then she walked up the plank leading to her office. The next night she did it all over again. She did it until it seemed to her that she was actually in a car; she could actually see herself in a car and riding the streets of San Francisco, stopping in front of her office building, getting out, thanking her driver, and then making her way up the ramp.

The second night, right after she had done it and given it the tones of reality, her companion read her the evening paper. And there in the evening paper was the picture of a man who was interested in blind people. Having read the article, she thought she would call him. She looked his name up in the telephone directory, and found his name and called him. He said he was interested in the blind, as said in the paper, but this was no time or place to call him. If she would write him a long, detailed letter of the nature of her problem he would take it under consideration. She sat down and wrote him a letter and explained her problem—simply a problem of transportation.

Next day when he got the letter he simply read it and put it in his pocket. On his way home he stopped in at a place where he stops every day before returning to his home. And that happened to be a bar. He stopped in at a bar. He knew the proprietor and had his little martini, or whatever he had, and while he was there he was prompted to tell the blind girl's story. Having told the story, a total stranger, who was a salesman for some liquor house, overhead the story. And he said, "Well, I make a good living and I do nothing for this community. Here is a girl who not only is taking herself off the backs of taxpayers, but in her letter she states that she is training nine other blind people to earn their own living. Here this girl, who should be supported by the taxpayers, earns her own living and she's taught nine others to earn their living; and I, who earn a wonderful living, I do nothing for our community. I will drive that girl to work."

The man who received the letter said, "If you, a total stranger, will drive her to work, I, who am interested in the blind and make it my job, I will then take her home. And that was the bargain. Now that's almost three years ago. I saw that girl just about six months ago and she told me that it has not failed one day of a five-day week. Five days a week, one gentleman picks her up and takes her to her work and one takes her from work to home. And here is the strange part. The very first morning that she drove with one of these men, she turned to him as she got out of the car, and she said, "Thank you very much, sir," to which he replied, "The pleasure is all mine." The identical words that she in her imagination had used to make the scene seem natural were used the very first day.

Now, it was twice she did it—on the third day she was being driven to work. I say to you if she can do it, and if the speaker can do it, you can do it. I have done it a number of times and I teach others to do it. It is a simple, simple technique. *You must learn to believe in the inner man and the reality of what is to you at the moment an invisible realm.* This invisible world is not *really* unreal; it's the most real world imaginable. And the inner man related to it is a far more real being than the outer personality that you cling to and think so much of in this world. *Try.* These things will never fail. Whenever the action of the inner you corresponds to the action that the outer you must take to appease your desire, that desire will be realized.

For this whole wonderful world around us is nothing more than the appeasement of hunger; that's why we built it. We made it to satisfy our longing. You have some intense longing, some wonderful hunger in this world, it may be for a job, it may be an increase of income, it may be some wonderful, harmonious relationship in a home that is now strained, no matter what it is, *construct a little act, this action inside, that your dream has been realized, then take that action and inwardly do it over and over and over until it takes on the tones of reality.* When to you it seems natural, then you may sleep. But I do believe in not sleeping during the action. In some strange way it seems to hinder the interval between the doing and the realization of it. Of course, you don't have to sleep. *But I have found from experience that if I can fall asleep while I am performing the action—the action that implies the fulfillment of my dream—that I quickly collapse the time.*

. . . This girl took maybe two days. Although she was driven on the third day, she really only did it two nights: two nights sitting in her living room she assumed she was in a car; she could smell the gasoline; she took all of her attention and hallucinated it—*you can hallucinate sights, smell, touch. I can take my hand now, place it on this book, and assume that I am fondling something that is not here to be seen by anyone.* And so lose myself in it that to me it seems natural. If I do it until it seems natural, and sleep while I'm doing it do you not think it will become my perception? That's how everyone should live and will eventually live in this world.

So instead of going out and simply grabbing things that are not yours or I would say stealing in order to survive, you don't steal to survive with this technique—you *die* in order to live. You let go of the things that you conceptualize, just drop them, and you simply inwardly see yourself into another state. And seeing yourself right into the situation of your fulfilled desire you sleep in that state. And so you know the wisdom of the word: "In a dream, in a vision of the night, when deep sleep falls upon men, in slumberings upon the bed, then he openeth the ears of men and sealeth their instructions."

We are rehearsed at night in the part that we are playing when we open our eyes in this outer world. And all that we will do we do under compulsion. For this inner motion is the force by which the outer event is brought to bear.

If you know it, then don't just know it—do it. For if you do it, I promise you, you will get the result. But you must apply it. Application is important. Everyone in this world must learn to live by their imagination. And only as you live by imagination can you truly be said to live at all. Now here in this book of mine, *Awakened Imagination,* you will find that case history of the blind girl. Read it and apply it. And become the man, the woman that you want to be. You can be anything in this world that you want to be; if you know these wonderful promises accept them and then test them. You're invited to test them. "Come prove me now and see if I will not open the windows of heaven and pour you out a blessing so great, there is not room on earth to receive it."

You can conceive of the impossible state—the impossible to the inner man. *All things are possible to the inner man.*

CHAPTER 15

"Inner Conversations"

Lecture, 1955

Talking to oneself is a habit everyone indulges in. We could no more stop talking to ourselves than we could stop eating and drinking. *All that we can do is control the nature and the direction of our inner conversations. Most of us are totally unaware of the fact that our inner conversations are the causes of the circumstance of our life.*

We are told that "as a man thinketh in his heart, so is he." But do we know that man's thinking follows the tracks laid down in his own inner conversations? To turn the tracks to which he is tied in the direction in which he wants to go, he must put off his former conversation, which is called in the Bible the Old Man, and be renewed in the spirit of his mind. *Speech is the image of mind; therefore, to change his mind, he must first change his speech.*

By "speech" is meant those mental conversations we carry on with ourselves.

The world is a magic circle of infinite possible mental transformations. For there are an infinite number of possible mental conversations. *When man discovers the creative power of inner talking, he will realize his function and his mission in life.* Then he can act to a purpose. Without such knowledge, he acts unconsciously. Everything is a manifestation of the mental conversations which go on in us without our being aware of them. But as civilized beings, we must become aware of them and act with a purpose.

A man's mental conversations attracts his life. As long as there is no change in his inner talking, the personal history of the man remains the same. To attempt to change the world before we change our inner talking is to struggle against the very nature of things. Man can go round and round in the same circle of disappointments and misfortunes, not seeing them as caused by his own negative inner talking, but as caused by others.

This may seem far-fetched, but it is a matter which lends itself to research and experiment. *The formula the chemist illustrates is not more certainly provable than the formula of this science by which words are clothed in objective reality.*

One day a girl told me of her difficulties in working with her employer. She was convinced that he unjustly criticized and rejected her very best efforts. Upon hearing her story, I explained that if she thought him unfair, it was a sure sign that she herself was in need of a new conversation piece. There was no doubt but that she was mentally arguing with her employer, for others only echo that which we whisper to them in secret.

She confessed that she argued mentally with him all day long. When she realized what she had been doing, she agreed to change her inner conversations with her employer. She imagined that he had congratulated her on her fine work, and that she in turn had thanked him for his praise and kindness. To her great delight, she soon discovered that her own attitude was the cause of all that befell her. The behavior of her employer reversed itself. It echoed, as it had always done, her mental conversations with him.

I rarely see a person alone without wondering, "to what conversation piece is he tied? On what mysterious track is he walking?" We must begin to take life consciously. For the solution of all problems lies just in this: the second man, the Lord from heaven in all of us, is trying to become self-conscious in the body, that he may be about his father's business. What are his labors? To imitate his father, to become master of the word, master of his inner talking, that he may mold this world of ours into a likeness with the Kingdom of Love.

The prophet said, "Be ye imitators of God as dear children." How would I imitate God? Well, we are told that God calls things that are not seen as though they were seen, and the unseen becomes seen. This is the way the girl called forth praise and kindness from her employer. She carried on an imaginary conversation with her employer from the premise that he had praised her work, and he did.

Our inner conversations represent in various ways the world we live in. Our individual worlds are self-revelations of our own inner speech. We are told that every idle word that men shall speak they shall give account thereof. For by their words they shall be justified, and by their words they shall be condemned.

We abandon ourselves to negative inner talking yet expect to retain command of life. *Our present mental conversations do not recede into the past as man believes. They advance into the future to confront us as wasted or invested words.* "My word," said the prophet, "shall not return unto me void, but it shall accomplish that which I please, and it shall prosper in all the things whereto I sent it."

How would I send my word to help a friend? I would imagine that I am hearing his voice, that he is physically present, that my hand is on him. I would then congratulate him on his good fortune, tell him that I have never seen him look better. I would listen as though I heard him; I would imagine that he is telling me he has never felt better, he has never been happier. And I would know that in this loving, knowing communion with another, a communion populous with loving thoughts and feelings, that my word was sent, and it shall not return unto me void, but it shall prosper in the thing whereto I sent it.

"Now is the accepted time, now is the day of salvation." It is only what is done now that counts, even though its effects may not be visible until tomorrow. We call, not out loud, but by an inner effort of intense attention; to listen attentively, as though you heard, is to create. The events and relationships of life are your Word made visible. *Most of us rob others of their willingness and their ability to be kind and generous by our fixed attitudes towards them.*

Our attitudes unfold within us in the form of mental conversations. *Inner talking from premises of fulfilled desire is the way to consciously create circumstances.*

Our inner conversations are perpetually outpictured all around us in happenings. Therefore, what we desire to see and hear without we must see and hear within, for the whole manifested world goes to show us what use we have made of the Word.

If you practice this art of controlled inner speaking, you too will know what a thrill it is to be able to say, "And now I have told you before it come to pass, that when it is come to pass, ye might believe." You will be able to consciously use your imagination to transform and channel the immense creative energies of your inner speech from the mental, emotional level to the physical level. And I do not know what limits, if any, there are to such a process.

What is your aim? Does your inner talking match it? It must, you know, if you would realize your aim. For as the prophet asked, "Can two walk together except they be agreed?" And of course the answer is, "No, they cannot." The two who must agree are your inner conversation and the state desired. That is, what you desire to see and hear without, you must see and hear within.

Every stage of man's progress is made by the conscious exercise of his imagination matching his inner speech to his fulfilled desire. As we control our inner talking, matching it to our fulfilled desires, we can lay aside all other processes. Then we simply act by clear imagination and intention: we imagine the wish fulfilled and carry on mental conversations from that premise. The right inner speech is the speech that would be yours were you to realize your ideal. In other words, it is the speech of fulfilled desire.

Now you will understand how wise the ancient was when he told us in the Hermetica, "There are two gifts which God has bestowed upon man alone and on no other mortal creature. These two are Mind and Speech, and the gift of Mind and Speech is equivalent to that of immortality. If a man uses these two gifts rightly, he will differ in nothing from the Immortals. And when he quits his body, Mind and Speech will be his guides, and by them he will be brought into the troop of the gods and the souls that have attained to bliss."

With the gift of mind and speech you create the conditions and circumstances of life. "In the beginning was the Word, and the Word was with God, and the Word was God." The Word, said Hermes, is Son, and Mind is Father of the Word. They are not separate one from the other, for life is the union of Word and Mind. You and your inner talking, or Word, are one. If your mind is one with your inner conversations, then to be transformed in mind is to be transformed in conversation.

It was a flash of the deepest insight that taught Paul to write: "Put off the former conversation, the old man which is corrupt, and be renewed in the spirit of your mind. Put on the new man." To "put on the new man" and "be renewed in the spirit of your mind," is to change your inner conversation, for speech and mind are one—*a change of speech is a change of mind.*

The prophet Samuel said, "The Lord spake by me, and his Word was in my tongue." If the Lord's Word was in the prophet's tongue, then the Lord's mouth that uttered the Word must be the prophet's mind, for inner conversations originate in the mind and produce little tiny speech movements in the tongue. The prophet is telling us that the mouth of God is the mind of man, that our inner conversations are the Word of God creating life about us as we create it within ourselves.

In the Bible you are told that the Word is very near to you, in your mouth and in your heart, that you may do it. "See, I have set before you this day life and good, death and evil, blessings and cursings. Choose life."

The conditions and circumstances of life are not created by some power external to yourself; they are the conditions which result from the exercise of your freedom of choice, your freedom to choose the ideas to which you will respond.

Now is the accepted time. This is the day of salvation. "Whatsoever things are of good report, think on these things." For your future will be formed by the Word of God which is your present inner talking. You create your future by your inner conversations. The worlds were framed by the Word of God, that is, your inner talking. "See yonder fields? The sesamum was sesamum, the corn was corn. The silence and the darkness knew! So is a man's fate born."

For ends run true to origins. If you would reap success, you must plant success. The idea in your mind which starts the whole process going is the idea which you accept as truth. This is a very important point to grasp, for truth depends upon the intensity of imagination, not upon "facts." When the girl imagined that her employer was unfair, his behavior confirmed her imagination. When she changed her assumption of him, his behavior reflected the change, proving that an assumption, though false, if persisted in will harden into fact.

The mind always behaves according to the assumption with which it starts. Therefore, to experience success, we must assume that we are successful. We must live wholly on the level of the imagination itself, and it must be consciously and deliberately undertaken. It does not matter if at the present moment external facts deny the truth of your assumption, if you persist in your assumption it will become a fact. *Signs follow, they do not precede.*

To assume a new concept of yourself is to that extent to change your inner talking or word of God and is, therefore, putting on the new man. *Our inner talking, though unheard by others, is more productive of future conditions than all the audible promises and threats of men.* Your ideal is waiting to be incarnated, but unless you yourself offer it human parentage it is incapable of birth. You must define the person you wish to be and then assume the feeling of your wish fulfilled in faith that that assumption will find expression through you.

The true test of religion is in its use, but men have made it a thing to defend. It is to you that the words are spoken, "Blessed is she that believed, for there shall be an accomplishment of those things which were spoken unto her from the Lord."

Test it. Try it. Conceive yourself to be one that you want to be and remain faithful to that conception, for life here is only a training ground for image making. Try it and see if life will not shape itself on the model of your imagination.

Everything in the world bears witness of the use or misuse of man's inner talking. Negative inner talking, particularly evil and envious inner talking, are the breeding ground of the future battlefields and penitentiaries of the world. Through habit man has developed the secret affection for these negative inner conversations. Through them he justifies failure, criticizes his neighbors, gloats over the distress of others, and in general pours out his venom on all. Such misuse of the word perpetuates the violence of the world.

The transformation of self requires that we meditate on a given phrase, a phrase which implies that our ideal is realized, and inwardly affirm it over and over and over again until we are inwardly affected by its implication, until we are possessed by it. Hold fast to your noble inner convictions or conversations.

Nothing can take them from you but yourself. Nothing can stop them from becoming objective facts. All things are generated out of your imagination by the Word of God, which is your own inner conversation. And every imagination reaps its own Words which it has inwardly spoken.

The great secret of success is a controlled inner conversation from premises of fulfilled desire. The only price you pay for success is the giving up of your former conversation which belongs to the old man, the unsuccessful man. The time is ripe for many of us to take conscious charge in creating heaven on earth. To consciously and voluntarily use our imagination, to inwardly hear and only say that which is in harmony with our ideal, is actively bringing heaven to earth.

Every time we exercise our imagination lovingly on behalf of another, we are literally mediating God to that one. Always use your imagination masterfully, as a participant, not an onlooker. In using your imagination to transform energy from the mental, emotional level to physical level, extend your senses—look and imagine that you are seeing what you want to see, that you are hearing what you want to hear, and touching what you want to touch. Become intensely aware of doing so. Give your imaginary state all the tones and feeling of reality. Keep on doing so until you arouse within yourself the mood of accomplishment and the feeling of relief.

This is the active, voluntary use of the imagination as distinguished from the passive, involuntary acceptance of appearances. It is by this active, voluntary use of the imagination that the second man, the Lord from heaven, is awakened in man.

Men call imagination a plaything, the "dream faculty." But actually it is the very gateway of reality.

Imagination is the way to the state desired, it is the truth of the state desired, and the life of that state desired. Could you realize this fully, then would you know that what you do in your imagination is the only important thing. Within the circle of our imagination the whole drama of life is being enacted over and over again. Through the bold and active use of the imagination we can stretch out our hand and touch a friend ten thousand miles away and bring health and wealth to the parched lips of his being. It is the way to everything in the world. How else could we function beyond our fleshly limitations? But imagination demands of us a fuller living of our dreams in the present.

Through the portals of the present the whole of time must pass. Imagine elsewhere as here, and then as now. Try it and see. You can always tell if you have succeeded in making the future dream a present fact by observing your inner talking. If you are inwardly saying what you would audibly say were you physically present and physically moving about in that place, then you have succeeded. And you could prophesy it from these inner conversations, and from the moods which they awaken within you, what your future will be.

For one power alone makes a prophet—the *imagination*, the divine vision. All that we meet is our word made visible. And what we do not now comprehend is related by affinity to the unrecognized forces of our own inner conversations and the moods which they arouse within us.

If we do not like what is happening to us, it is a sure sign that we are in need of a change of mental diet. For man, we are told, lives not by bread alone but by every word that proceeds from the mouth of God. And having discovered the mouth of God to be the mind of man, a mind which lives on words or inner talking, we should feed into our minds only loving, noble thoughts. For with words or inner talking we build our world.

Let love's lordly hand raise your hunger and thirst to all that is noble and of good report, and let your mind starve e'er you raise your hand to a cup love did not fill or a bowl love did not bless. That you may never again have to say, "What have I said? What have I done, O All Powerful Human Word?"

CHAPTER 16

"The Secret of Imagining"

From vinyl record, Neville, 1960

... Nothing appears or continues in being by a power of its own. Events happen because comparatively stable imaginable activities created them. And they continue in being only as long as they receive such support. Therefore the secret of imagining is the greatest of all problems, to the solution of which everyone should aspire. For supreme power, supreme wisdom, and supreme joy lie in the solution of this great mystery. When man solves the mystery of imagining he will have discovered the secret of causation, and that is: *imagining creates reality.*

Divine imagining and human imagining are not two powers at all but one. The valid distinction which exists between them lies not in the sub-

stance with which they operate, but in the degree of intensity of the operant power itself. Acting at high tension, an imaginable act is an immediate objective fact. Keyed low, an imaginable act is realized in a time process.

Human history, with its forms of governments, its revolutions, it wars, and in fact the rise and fall of nations, could be written in terms of the imaginal activities of men and women. *All imaginative men and women are forever casting forth enchantments, and all passive men and women, who have no powerful imaginative lives, are continually passing under the spell of their power.* If imagination is the only thing that acts or is in existing beings or men, as Blake believed, then we should never be certain that it was not some woman treading in the wine press who began that subtle change in men's minds. Or that the passion, because of which the earth has been drenched in blood, did not begin in the imagination of some shepherd boy lighting up his eye for a moment before it ran upon its way.

The future is the imaginable activity of man in its creative march. Imagining is the creative power, not only of the poet, the artist, the actor, and orator, but of the scientist, the inventor, the merchant, and the artisan. Its abuse in unrestrained, unlovely image making is obvious. But its abuse in undue repression breeds a sterility, which robs a man of actual wealth of experience. *Imagining novel solutions to ever more complex problems is far more noble than to restrain or kill out desire. Life is the continuing solution of a continuously synthetic problem.* Imagining creates events. Our world, created out of men's imagining, comprise unnumbered warring beliefs. Therefore there could never be a perfectly stable or static state. *Today's events are bound to disturb yesterday's established order. Imaginative men and women invariably unsettle a preexisting peace of mind.*

Hold fast to your ideal in your imagination. Nothing can take it from you but your failure to persist in imagining the ideal realized. Imagine only such states that are of value or promise well. *To attempt to change circumstances before we change our imaginal activity is to struggle against the very nature of things. There can be no outer change until there is first an imaginal change. Everything we do unaccompanied by an imaginal change is but futile readjustment of services.* Imagining the wish fulfilled brings about a union with that state. And during that union we behave in keeping with our imaginal change. This shows us that an imaginal change will result in a change of behavior. However, our ordinary imaginal alterations, as we pass from one state to another, are not transformations. Because each of them is so rapidly succeeded by another in the reverse direction; but whenever one state grows so stable as to become our constant mood, our habitual attitude, then that habitual state defines our character and is a true transformation . . .

. . . *Man, through the medium of a controlled waking dream, can predetermine his future. That imaginal activity, of living in the feeling of the wish fulfilled, leads man across a bridge of incident to the fulfillment of the dream.*

If we live in the dream, thinking from it and not of it, then the creative power of imagining will answer our adventurous fancy and the wish fulfilled will break in upon us and take us unawares. Man is all imagination; therefore man must be where he is in imagination, for his imagination is himself.

To realize that imagination is not something tied to the senses, or enclosed within the spatial boundary of the body, is most important. Although man moves about in space by movement of his physical body he need not be so restricted. He can move by a change in what he's aware of. However real the scene on which sight rests, man can gaze on one never before witnessed. He can always remove the mountain if it upsets his concept of what life ought to be. This ability to mentally move from things as they are to things as they ought to be is one of the most important discoveries that man can make. It reveals man as a center of imagining with powers of intervention, which enable him to alter the course of observed events, moving from success to success through a series of mental transformations of nature, of others, and himself.

How does he do it? Self-abandonment. That is the secret. He has to abandon himself mentally to his wish fulfilled, in his love for that state, and in so doing live in the new state and no more in the old state.

Now we can't commit ourselves to what we do not love. So the secret of self-commission is faith plus love. Faith is believing what is incredible. We commit ourselves to the feeling of the wish fulfilled in faith that this act of self-commission will become a reality—and it will because imagining creates reality.

Imagination is both conservative and transformative. It is conservative when it builds its world from images supplied by memory and the evidence of the senses. It is creatively transformative when it imagines things as they ought to be, building its world out of the generous dreams of fancy. In the procession of images, the ones that take precedence naturally are those of the senses. Nevertheless, a present sense impression is only an image; it does not differ in nature from a memory image or the image of a wish. What makes a present sense impression so objectively real is the individual's imagination functioning in it and thinking from it. Whereas in a memory image or a wish, the individual's imagination is not functioning in it or thinking from it but is functioning out of it and thinking of it. If the individual would enter into the image in his imagination... then would he know what it is to be creatively transformative, then would he realize his wish, and then he would be happy.

Every image can be embodied, but unless man himself enters the image and thinks from it, it is incapable of birth. Therefore it is the height of folly to expect the wish to be realized by the mere passage of time. That which requires imaginative occupancy to produce its effect obviously cannot be affected without such occupancy. We cannot be in one image and not suffer the consequences of not being in another. Imagination is spiritual sensation. Enter the image of the wish fulfilled, then give it sensory vividness and tones of reality by mentally acting as you would act were it a physical fact.

Now this is what I mean by spiritual sensation. *Imagine that you are holding a rose in your hand. Smell it. Do you detect the odor of roses? Well if the rose is not here why is its fragrance in the air? Through spiritual sensation—that is, through imaginal sight, sound, scent, taste, and touch— man can give to the image sensory vividness. If he does, all things will conspire to aid his harvesting. And on reflection he will see how subtle were the threads that led to his goal. He could never have devised the means which his imaginal activity used to fulfill itself.* If man longs to escape from his present sense fixation, to transform his present life into a dream of what might well be, he has but to imagine that he's already what he wants to be, and then feel the way he would expect to feel under such circumstances. Let him, like the make believe of a child, who is remaking the world after its own heart, create his world out of pure dreams of fancy. Let him mentally enter into his dream. Let him mentally do what he would actually do were it physically true. He will discover that dreams are realized not by the rich but by the imaginative.

Nothing stands between man and the fulfillment of his dream but facts, and facts are the creations of imagining.* If man changes his imag-

———————————

* Given the tenor of our political moment as I assemble this collection in the early summer of 2020, I hope readers will not mind the addition of a personal note to this passage. Neville writes, "Nothing stands between man and the fulfillment of his dream but facts, and facts are the creations of imagining." Is that a beautiful ideal—or a formula for corruption?

Several journalists and historians, myself included, have noted the connection between New Thought and Donald Trump, who acknowledges the influence of *The Power of Positive Thinking* by Rev. Norman Vincent Peale. Some critics complain that Trump's "reality distortion" has produced disastrous effects, all of it abetted by statements like the one above, which Trump encountered in adulterated form in the work of Peale.

I wrestle with this question. I am, of course, dedicated to Neville's work; but I have no right to disassemble another's life based

ining he will change the facts. Man and his past are one continuous structure. This structure contains all of the facts which have been conserved and still operate below the threshold of his surface mind. For him, it is merely history. For him, it seems unalterable: a dead and firmly fixed past. But for itself it is living; it is part of the living age. We cannot leave behind us the mistakes of our past, for nothing disappears. Everything that has been is still in existence. The past still exists, and it gives and still gives its results. Man must go back in memory, seek for and destroy the causes of evil however far back they lie. This going into the past and replaying a scene of the past in imagination as it ought to have been played the first time, I call revision—and revision results in repeal. Changing our lives means changing the past. The causes of the present evil are the unrevised scenes of the past. The past and the present form the whole structure of man. It is carrying all of its

---

on my assumptions. In this regard, I find guidance in the work of Ralph Waldo Emerson, who wrote in his journals of January 15, 1857: "This good which invites me now is visible & specific. I will at least embrace it this time by way of experiment, & if it is wrong certainly God can in some manner signify his will in future. Moreover I will guard against evil consequences resulting to others by the vigilance with which I conceal it."

In other words, my experiments are wholly intimate; I take any risk upon myself alone. This supplies the inner meaning of the dictum to be "wise as serpents and harmless as doves."—MH

contents with it. Any alteration of content will result in an alteration in the present and future.

Live nobly, so that mind can store a past well worthy of recall. Should you fail to do so, remember, the first act of correction or cure is always: *revise*. If the past is recreated into the present, so will the revised past be recreated into the present. Or else the promise that "though you sins are like scarlet, they shall be as white as snow," is a lie.

The question may arise as to how by representing others to ourselves as better than they really were, or mentally rewriting a letter to make it conform to our wish, or by revising the scene of an accident, the interview with the employer, and so on, could change what seems to be the unalterable facts of the past—but remember my claims for imagining. Imagining creates realty. What it makes it can unmake. It is not only conservative, building a life from images supplied by memory; it is always creatively transformative, altering a theme already in being. The parable of the unjust steward gives the answer to this question. We can alter our world by means of a certain illegal practice, by means of a falsification of the facts; that is, by means of a certain intentional alteration of that which we have experienced. And all this is done in one's own imagination. This is a form of falsehood, which is not only is not condemned, but is actually approved in the gospel teaching. By means of such of falsehood, a man destroys the causes of evil and acquires friends. And on the strength of this revision proves, judging by the high praise the unjust steward received from his master, that he is deserving of confidence.

Because imagining creates reality we can carry revision to the extreme, and revise a scene that would be otherwise unforgivable. We learn to distinguish between man, who is all imagination, from those states into which he may enter. An unjust steward, looking at another's distress, will represent the other to himself as he ought to be seen. Were he himself in need he would, like the man on the cover of this record, enter his dream house in his imagination and imagine what he would see, and how things would seem, and how people would act, after these things should be. Then in this state he would fall asleep feeling the way he would expect to feel under such circumstances.

Would that all the Lord's people were unjust stewards, mentally falsifying the facts of life to deliver individuals forever more. For the imaginal change goes forward until at length the altered pattern is realized on the heights of attainment. Our future is our imaginal activity in its creative march. Imagine better than the best you know.

CHAPTER 17

"Election and Change of Consciousness"

Lecture, February 24, 1963

Election is an act of God, not based upon any inherent superiority of those elected, but grounded in the love and grace of God and in his promises to the Father. Let no one boast who is called. Let no one boast who is elected, for all will be called, but in God's own predetermined time. So tonight my subject is "Election and Change of Consciousness."

God speaks to man through the medium of dream and reveals himself in vision, and we are past masters of misinterpreting his words. *A dream is a parable containing a single jet of truth. Don't try to give meaning to every word or event of the dream. Perhaps there will be several dreams, several stories in a single dream—then each story contains its own jet of truth.* Let me share one such dream of a friend. Her dream is in three parts. It is a wonderful dream on the higher level. The lady states:

I found myself in an old, comfortable farmhouse. Outside an old horse grazed in the sun and an old dog slept under a tree. Suddenly a man appeared at my door and said: "You have been chosen and must leave this place." For a moment I panicked. What would I do about the house and the animals outside? Perhaps I could sell them or give them away. Then the man, having read my thoughts, said: "No, you cannot sell them or give them away. You must leave them as they are, and your leaving must be voluntary."

The moment I chose to leave, the scene changed and I am in an entirely different world, talking to a man and a woman. They tell me that I must play three games, of which two have been completed, although I couldn't remember playing them. Now standing in the center of a beautiful green field, I see an enormous mountain in the distance. I am told that I must run across this field, gather anything I can along the way, and reach the top of the mountain in ten seconds. Then I must interpret what I have accomplished along the way. Scooping up a few stones, I began to run, stopping occasionally to gather more stones along the way. When I reached the top of the mountain I discovered my stones had become golden nuggets which had fused together. Extending my hand for those who were there to see, I said: "This is my mind of golden wisdom" and they replied: "You have found the way."

Then the dream changed and I am standing gazing at a child lying in a crib. Its head appeared to be indented, as though it had been lying on rocks or sand. Rubbing the child's head, I smoothed its skin and it smiled. Then I dressed it, made it more comfortable, and as I was feeding it I awoke, still seeing the smile on its face.

God spoke to this lady in a glorious dream. *A house is the symbol of the state from which you abide. Hers was very comfortable. A dog is the symbol of faith. Called Caleb, in Scripture, he is the one who crossed the river with Joshua. He is called the hound of faith. Now, a horse is the symbol of the mind. In her case he represented a comfortable way of thinking.*

Then the man appears to tell her she is chosen. *In Scripture, God's messenger is always the Lord himself, for "my name is in him."* So the Lord appeared, not as some strange creature from outer space or as an impersonal force, but as an ordinary man. He tells her she is chosen. Chosen to leave this age. She cannot sell or give her present state of consciousness away. She must voluntarily leave it for another to occupy.

Entering an entirely different age, she meets two, and there is conflict until she reaches the mountain top where the God in her reveals the mind of golden wisdom. Now, in Paul's last letter to Timothy, he says: "The time of my departure has come." Then he mentions three events, saying: "I have fought the good fight. I have finished the race. I have kept the faith." Like Paul, she has fought the good fight and finished the race, for she has kept the faith—just as everyone will—for it is God who is doing it all.

Then she finds wisdom, personified as a little child, he who said: "Before he created the heavens I stood beside him as a little child. I was daily his delight, rejoicing constantly before him and delighting in the affairs of men. Listen to me carefully. He who finds me finds life. He who misses me injures himself. He who hates me, loves death." She found the child. She found life. Animating bodies in this world of death, we are destined to become life-giving spirits by finding life. Having won the race, having kept the faith, having fought the good fight, she has found the child. *Don't be concerned about all the little pieces of a dream; simply see the symbols present there.*

Now let me repeat once again: *Scripture is not history, and the characters depicted there are not persons, but personifications of eternal states of consciousness.* We all started this journey into death in the state of Abraham. In the 23rd chapter of Genesis it is said that Sarah dies and Abraham becomes a sojourner in a strange land for 400 years. Called the father of the multitude, God promised Abraham that he would return, bringing all with him. Going to the Hittites, Abraham tells them he has no land to bury his wife, and they say: "Hear us, my lord; you are a mighty prince among us. Take the choicest of our sepulchers; none will withhold his sepulcher from you, or hinder you from burying your dead."

May I tell you: every child born of woman is God the Father, buried in the sepulcher of the Hittites, called Canaanites. Every black man, every white man, every nationality, race or creed born of woman is a Canaanite where God the Father is buried. This was a deliberate act, not a punishment. Listen to the words in the 82nd Psalm: "God has taken his place in the divine council where he holds judgment saying: 'You are gods, sons of the Most High, all of you; nevertheless, you will die like men and fall as one man, O princes.'" *We are the ones who deliberately fell into these garments, these sepulchers. A god is entombed in every skull. You didn't begin in your mother's womb. You are buried in the body your mother wove for you, and from that sepulcher you will be called in fulfillment of God's promise.*

So let me repeat: Election is an act of God, not based on any inherent superiority of those elected, but grounded in the love and the grace of God and in his promises to the Father. It is to the Father that the promise is made. Everyone has been promised that he will die and will be raised from that state. Everyone will be called from the age of death to once again enter the age of everlasting life. This lady has been called. She has been chosen and all the events recorded in scripture will take place in her.

It thrills me beyond measure to know that in this small circle so many are being called. Everyone will be called, for God is in them and God cannot fail to lift himself up in everyone. Having played all the states, as everyone must, you will have kept the faith and God will keep his promise and lift himself up, in you, just as he laid himself down in you.

It is the God in you who said: "No one takes my life, I lay it down myself. I have the power to lay it down and the power to lift it up again." As God's power is lifted up in you, you depart this age.

Now, in another's dream, he is driving his wife's car over a mountainous road. Suddenly the hair on the back of his head catches fire and he turns and rubs his head against the back of the seat to put out the fire. But in so doing, he loses control of the car and it goes over the cliff in slow motion. Seeing that the fall is about 300 feet, he opens the door of the car and jumps, saying to himself "This is a dream. I AM!" With that thought in mind he descends to the ground below as light and softly as a flake of snow, and awakes on his bed, saying to himself: "I have had this dream three times, and each time I have written it to Neville, but this is the first time I have awakened in the dream."

What is the single jet of truth in this dream? He is riding in his wife's car. A wife is that to which I AM is attached. A state which bears my name. There are infinite states in this world and when you enter a state you are wedded to it. The state may be one of luxury or ill health, the state of being ignored or famous; but any state is God's emanation, his wife. *The dream denotes a departure from the state in which the God in him has been residing, into an entirely different state. Perhaps he is presently wedded to a state in which he is making $10,000 a year and he desires to live in the state of earning $40,000 or even $100,000. There's nothing wrong with that. Every state is a garment, ready and waiting for you to slip on, and you're free to wear—and thereby marry—any state you like.*

If you want to be important in the eyes of shadows, you can; but when the God in you awakes all the shadows will vanish and you will return enhanced and glorified to the being that you were prior to your descent into death, for this is the world of death. Everything here appears, it waxes, it wanes, and it vanishes. *You do not die when men call you dead. You are still clothed in the same garment, but younger than you were when you made your exit, to again wax, wane, and vanish, to repeat the act over and over again.* This is what the Bible teaches. Read the 20th chapter of the Book of Luke: "The sons of this age marry and are given in marriage; but those who are accounted worthy to attain to that age neither marry nor are given in marriage, for they cannot die anymore."

There are two distinct ages. We remain in this age, experiencing states over and over again until we are elected and called to enter that age. And because you are so unique you are called one by one, for no one can take your place. You are a part of the body of God, the God who deliberately fell. The God who, reaching the limit of contraction, buried himself in his chosen sepulcher (your skull), from which he will rise as promised in the beginning. "I say, ye are gods, sons of the Most High, all of you." Not just a few, but all of you. "Nevertheless, you will die like men and fall as one man, O princes." Now I say to you, O mighty princes: the sepulcher you chose was paid for by 400 shekels of silver. Four hundred, in Hebrew, carries the sign of the cross. The price God paid to become you.

When Abraham entered the sepulcher, becoming a Hittite, God died by completely forgetting who I AM. He didn't pretend, but buried himself in your skull and died, there to remain until I AM born from above. Then memory returns. *But until that time, no matter what position he plays in the world, he does not know who he is. You can be the wisest of the wise, the strongest of the strong, and still not know who you are until God awakens in you.* "He has taken the foolish to shame the wise. He has taken the weak to shame the strong. He has taken those who are low and despised, even things that are not, to bring to nothing things that are."

Jesus Christ is defined as the power of God and the wisdom of God. "He is our source, having been made our wisdom, our righteousness and our redemption." God's own power is Christ Jesus. His own wisdom is Christ Jesus, and he has made Christ Jesus your wisdom and your redemption; therefore Christ in you is the hope of glory, for when Christ returns, God has gathered his creative power and wisdom back unto himself—that power and wisdom which was buried in man.

My friend, in her vision, brought her golden nuggets back to the top of the mountain, where all of her experiences in the world of death were gathered together and fused into the one mind of golden wisdom. So God enhances himself; having reached the limit of contraction he expands. Having reached the limit of opacity he becomes translucent; therefore, he is far greater than he was when he fell into the Hittite.

When a little child is born, he lives because God buried himself in him. Do not think that because someone is going to the gas chamber tonight he is less than you are. *Do not allow anyone to pull his rank on you either, for no one is important in this world. There is no one but God who is buried in every person in the world, and every person is equal.* So let me repeat: election is an act of God, not based upon any inherent superiority of those elected, but grounded in the love and grace of God and in his promises to the Father. Everyone was promised that he would be redeemed, and God has kept his promise.

Christ Jesus in me is God's power and wisdom, and when redeemed, I am he, for everything said of him I have experienced. *I still wear a garment called Neville, but I have awakened to another age. I am still the same man in the world of Caesar. I still sign my name on my checks, and the shadows who receive them can exchange them for more shadows based on my signature.* But the being that is called into an entirely different world was before the beginning but is enhanced now because of the experience. So everyone is richer for coming into this world, for God's creative power has been enhanced.

The child she saw is a symbol of her trans-formed creative power. She has experienced a change of age. But the man experienced a change of state. I can tell him tonight that the dream doesn't mean he is departing this world. He has a wife to support and little children to educate. The dream has nothing to do with breaking his neck here, or divorcing his wife, for he is not married to her, but to a state in this world. He leaves a state and enters another—be it noble or ignoble—for he was driving his wife's car when he awoke to realize it was a dream.

Now, in the waking dream you can learn to control your imagination so that you can set in motion your status from one level to another, but you cannot change the age. That comes out of the blue. That comes when you least expect it. *No one can earn the exit from this age. That comes upon you suddenly, as promised in the beginning. So let no one boast and tell you they earned the kingdom. We are all put through the furnaces for his own sake, for his name he cannot give to another.* It is yours, as promised, before the beginning of the world. "I came out from the Father and came into the world. Again I am leaving the world and returning to the Father." *Here is pre-existence, incarnation, departure, and pre-destination.* It takes not just three-score-and-ten, but a long, long while. *And the pigment of your skin, your social or intellectual position, has nothing to do with your departure from this age.*

If you want the shadow of worldly fame you may have it, but it will not aid you in waking from the dream of life. If you will fall in love with what I am talking about, and set your heart fully upon the grace that is coming to you at the unveiling of Jesus Christ in you, you are on the verge. But if that doesn't interest you, and more money does, then get more money. If you want more cash, more fame, whatever you desire—get them, for they are all shadows. A big home is a big shadow, and a little home a little shadow, so it doesn't really matter . . .

. . . Everything is a state which is real, yet invisible. Not knowing this, and seeing no evidence to support your desired state, you may return to the former one. Expecting the new state to happen now, you don't remain faithful to it. But if you will remain there until it becomes natural to think from that state, it will be born in your world. *There is a period of time between your entrance into the invisible state and its visibility, and it has to come. Everything has an interval of time. The vision has its own appointed hour. If it seems long, wait. It is sure and it will not be late.* A little sheep takes five months, a man nine months, a horse one year. All these are fixed intervals of time.

How long will it take for a state to become objective? As long as it takes the nature of that seed to hatch. All you are called upon to do is to go into the state and remain there psychologically. Although you will continue to physically walk the earth as one person, as you think from your desired psychological state, it takes on physical tones and becomes a fact in your world. This is how you move from state to state as you wait for the promise of God to fulfill itself.

On that day you will be called and incorporated into his immortal body to express a far greater translucency and expansion than you knew prior to the start of your journey into the world of death. I can't tell you the thrill that is in store for you when you experience the embrace of love. There are no words to describe it, but as you embrace, you fuse to become one body, one Spirit, yet without loss of identity. Everyone will be called into that same union. Everyone will experience the end of the journey, for not one will be lost in all my holy mountain.

CHAPTER 18

"The World of Caesar"

Lecture, October 23, 1967

... You have come into this world only to finish the work of him who sent you. And who is he? The Father. "He who sees me, sees he who sent me. I came out from the Father and came into the world. Again I leave the world and return to the Father. He who sees me sees the Father, for I and the Father are one."

Conceiving the thought in the beginning, God had to have an agent to express it. *Everything in this world needs man to express it and may I tell you: God is man.* In the beginning God made man in his image. "Male/female made he them and called their name Man." Read it carefully in the 5th chapter of Genesis. Creating Man to express himself, God comes into the world to express and finish what he conceived in the beginning. Conceiving a state and knowing it takes a man to express it; God sent himself from the depth of his own being into this world to fulfill the state . . .

. . . We are told in the 22nd chapter of the Book of Luke: "Scripture must be fulfilled in me," so you must be about your Father's business by experiencing everything said of Jesus Christ in scripture. The miraculous birth will be yours, the discovery of the Fatherhood, the ascent into heaven and the descent of the Holy Spirit upon you in the bodily form of a dove. Then like the psalmist you will say: "Thou hast delivered me from the world of death," for you will know from experience that in the volume of the book it was all about you! . . .

. . . On this level you can be rich if that is your desire but remember *the story of Jesus is persistent assumption.* You can persist in the assumption that you are wealthy. I have many friends across this country who are very, very wealthy, yet I would say ninety-nine percent of them are miserable; but they will all tell you the same thing. I think of one in particular now. She has a fortune in diamonds. Tiffany, who sells diamonds marked up 300-400%, offered her $100,000 for one piece. When she joins us for dinner in New York City she wears a broach, a ring, and a pendant, worth a half million dollars. Ruth was born a very poor girl and—desiring wealth—she persistently assumed she was married to tremendous wealth. She had no money. Her only claim to any social status was that she was a descendant of the Adams who were in the White House. He, on the other hand, came out of a line of rascals. His great-grandfather was a bishop in New York; therefore, had good advice as to his descent and how to guard it. Ruth married and lived in hell for twenty-odd years, bearing him three sons. Now well into her seventies, her only desire is to marry more wealth and have more diamonds.

That is all right. The story of Jesus is a complete and undeviating persistence in the assumption that you are what you want to be. *If you haven't experienced wealth and that is what you want, persistently assume: "I am wealthy." If you have not experienced fame, assume you are famous, but, "The day will come," saith the Lord "when I will send a famine upon you. It will not be a hunger for bread or a thirst for water, but for the hearing of my Word." If that hunger hasn't come to you, then take the same story of Jesus and fulfill your every desire.*

When I am in New York, my friend comes to every meeting. She is a delightful person, but she is brutally honest with her desires. She wants more and more diamonds, more emeralds, more museum pieces. She confessed that she had no hunger to hear anything about David, but wants more and more money to leave her two sons. She wants more and more worldly illusions; but it is my hope that the hunger has come to you who are here—not for more and more bread and water, but for hearing the word of God with understanding . . .

. . . You want to be rich? That's the story of Jesus, which is a persistent assumption in the conviction that "I am rich," for unless you believe that "I am rich" you die in your sins and continue to claim, "I am poor." You want to be known? Then persistently assume: "I am known." Want to be healthy? "I am healthy!" Regardless of what you want to be, you must declare you already are it and persist in that assumption. An assumption is an act of faith, and without faith it is impossible to please God. Your reasoning mind may deny wealth. Your senses deny it too, but if you have faith you will dare to assume wealth, thereby becoming the man you want to be.

Maybe, tonight you would rather continue to worship a Jesus Christ on the outside. Maybe you would rather continue to walk with the sheep of the world and not be the shepherd, but you would like to feed on green pastures by still waters, instead of climbing the steep hills of doubt and fear as most people do. You can, if you will persistently assume: "I am well fed. I am wanted. I am known and every-thing is as I want it to be." But remember: to bring all these things into being, there must be a persistent assumption. That's the story of Jesus.

Now we are told in Jeremiah that God's word will not turn back until he has executed and accomplished the intents of his mind, which is that you become God. "In the later days you will understand it clearly." It is God's purpose to give himself to man and he will not turn back until he has executed and accomplished the intents of his mind. *So in the final days he sends a hunger unto your heart—not for bread, a larger home or jewelry—but for the hearing of the Word of God.* When this hunger possesses you, nothing will satisfy you but an experience of God. And if it is God's purpose to give you himself as himself, when you have experienced his Word you are God! . . ."

. . . I came into the world completely forgetful of the being that I AM. I had to. When I first met my friend Abdullah back in 1931 I entered a room where he was speaking and when the speech was ended he came over, extended his hand and said: "Neville, you are six months late." I had never seen the man before, so I said: "I am six months late? How do you know me?" and he replied: "The brothers told me that you were coming and you are six months late."

I was late because the one who told me of Abdullah was a Catholic priest. I loved him dearly, but I thought he was almost a moron. His father, a rum-runner in the days of prohibition, left him two million dollars, which he proceeded to lose on Wall

Street the first year. The only wonderful thing he did was to take the last $15,000 and give it to a Catholic organization to care for his mother the rest of her earthly days. So, having no respect for his judgment, when he told me about Abdullah I postponed going to hear him until one day I could find no excuse. When Ab called me by name I said: "I don't know you," and he replied: "Oh yes you do, but you have forgotten. We were together in China thousands of years ago, but you promised to completely forget in order to play the part you must play now." . . .

. . . You who are here are hungry for the Word of God. You are thirsty for the Word of God. You could be at home this night watching TV and it would cost you nothing, but you have given up your time and your money to be here because of your hunger. I have been sent to tell you not only that you become God when he is fulfilled in you, but how to cushion the blows in this world of reason by delighting in his law. His law is simply a persistent assumption in the claim: "I am what I want to be." Do not judge one who does not have the hunger for the Word of God, but tell him how to become what he wants to be.

Tell him that the story of Jesus is a *perpetual, persistent assumption* in whatever he wants to be. That Christ in him is the power of God and his imagination is that power and wisdom. Tell him that imagination knows how to bring his assumption to pass, but that he must persist.

Now I ask you: are you willing to persist in the assumption that you are what you want to be? Or are you going to go home tonight and say: "That was a nice little talk he gave, but after all he has a million dollars in the bank and I have nothing." If you think that, you are disobedient, for by that thought you have lack of faith in "I Am He!" That's the fundamental sin of the universe. There are only two sins recorded in scripture that offend God. One is: "Unless you believe that I Am He you die in your sins," and the other is eating of the fruit of tree of knowledge of good and evil. Ask our generals tonight if it would be good to stop bombing Vietnam and they would say, No. Go across the ocean and ask the Vietnamese and they would say, Yes. So what is good and what is evil?

I am not asking anyone but you! What would be good for you? Tell me, because in the end every conflict will resolve itself as *the world is simply mirroring the being you are assuming that you are.* One day you will be so saturated with wealth, so saturated with power in the world of Caesar, you will turn your back on it all and go in search for the Word of God. I remember when I had so much wealth. I did not have one home, but many, each fully staffed from secretaries to gardeners. That was a life of sheer decadence. I recall walking out of it and not returning. Whether they ever found the body I do not know, but I do know I deliberately walked away. Then about ten years ago in one of my journeys in spirit, I walked back into the world and saw it just as it was before. Strangely enough, everyone recognized me and welcomed me with open arms, but I stayed only for a moment then returned here bringing with me its vivid memory. *So I do believe that one must completely saturate himself with the things of Caesar before he is hungry for the Word of God.*

I am convinced you are here because of your hunger. I know you have obligations to society, you must pay Caesar's debts, so you want more money, but your hunger is greater for the hearing of the Word of God than for things of Caesar. That is why you are here, and you are blessed by it.

CHAPTER 19

"It Will Not be Late"

Lecture, March 15, 1968

. . . There are those who try to rush everything into being. They try to force birth from conception, but it cannot be done. There are many experiences not recorded in Scripture, and I am not here to stand in judgment of anyone as to whether they have experienced Scripture or not. But I do know from experience that on this level, *if you dare to assume you are what you want to be, your inner conviction, your feeling of certainty will bring it to pass. When you embrace the desired state, you have assumed its impregnation, and its fulfillment has its own appointed hour. It will ripen and flower. If the state is slow in objectifying itself wait, for it is sure and will not be late . . .*

. . . Ask no one if you are entitled to it or if you did it—only you know what you did. It happened to you.

Now wait for the vision (the desire's fulfillment) for it has its own appointed hour. It ripens, it will flower. *If it seems long then wait, for it is sure and it will not be late ...*

... We are told in the 15th chapter of Genesis that "You and your descendants will be enslaved for four hundred years." Now, the number four hundred is the twenty-second letter of the Hebrew alphabet whose symbol is the cross. Your body (of beliefs) is the cross referred to as four hundred, and as long as you wear it you are enslaved in a land that is not yours. *But in the end you will be brought out with great possessions!*

In the 12th chapter of Exodus, thirty years has been added to the four hundred, and in the New Testament it is said that Jesus began his ministry when he was about thirty years of age. In this world you are enslaved, *and here you remain playing your part until you are embraced, impregnated, and thirty years later Christ is born in you and your trials and tribulations are over!* So four hundred does not mean years, but thirty does. Four hundred records the length which Blake calls 6,000 or 8,500 years. Call it what you will, it is the period of time man plays his part in this world. Then comes the moment when, as Man, you are selected, called and embraced, and told to stand upon your watch; for the sign has its own appointed time to ripen and to flower, and that time is thirty years! . . .

. . . I do not know how long it takes for each egg to hatch in a nest, but I do know each one will hatch in its own time. And so it is with an assumption. If I desire to be wealthy, I may not know how long it will take me to reach the conviction that I possess great wealth, but when I feel wealth is mine I have conceived. *Conception is my end. The length of time between my desire and its conception depends entirely upon my inner conviction that it is done. A horse takes twelve months, a cow nine months, a chicken twenty-one days, so there are intervals of time; but it comes down to the simple fact that the truth concerning every concept is known by the feeling of its certainty.* When you know it, not a thing can disturb your knowingness! . . .

. . . Unfortunately we do not keep an account to see how long it takes to come about after we have done it. But a concept is an egg and remains so until occupied. Occupy your desire! Feel its certainty and you can prophesy its fulfillment.

Although I did not know what would become of it, I kept a record of what happened to me in 1929,*

---

* Neville is referencing an experience he described in *The Law and the Promise* (1961): "Many years ago, I was taken in spirit into a Divine Society, a Society of men in whom God is awake. Though it may seem strange, the gods do truly meet."—MII

so when I was born from above and raised from within myself in 1959, I looked back to discover that it was thirty years. I discovered that Jesus began his ministry when he was thirty years of age, and that Israel made their exodus thirty years after the four hundred recorded in Genesis. We are going to celebrate this exodus in the immediate future as the Passover, "a day to keep in memory forever." For "this is a night of watching by the Lord. On this day the Lord will bring the entire host of Israel out of the land of Egypt" and they will come out one by one. So if someone tells me a story that is not part of my experience, I cannot confirm it or deny it; I only know that my experiences parallel scripture.

But I say to you: *everything has its own appointed time. It ripens and will flower. If fulfillment seems long, wait, for it is sure and will not be late. Everything comes on time, but we do not know the time interval because we do not record the conception.* In my case, I keep a diary. I check scripture to find out where the passage is that I have experienced and record the date beside it. Now I know the length of time it takes to fulfill Scripture. I also know that when it comes to the world of Caesar, I have received confirmation while in the silence. I have exploded right into the now and, having felt the thrill I knew it had to happen, but I did not know when. It could be a day, a week, or a month. Three weeks ago I heard good news for a friend, and today I received confirmation that it was completed. I will not catalog that event to say that particular desire equals all desires, because a desire can be as different as a chicken's egg is from the egg of an elephant. I do know, however that events of Scripture do have definite time periods. Scripture fulfills itself in God's time, and *you cannot delay it or hasten its coming . . .*

. . . *Tonight I ask you to take the most fantastic thing in this world and find an inner conviction within yourself that it is yours, for the truth of any concept is known by the feeling of certainty which that conviction inspires.* Once you have that inner feeling of certainty, don't ask me to confirm it. What would it matter what I think? Do not be disillusioned if your experience has not been mine. Believe in yourself and trust your inner feeling. Test yourself and if it works on this level it will work in the depths of your being . . .

. . . You can always tell the truth of any concept by the feeling of certainty which it inspires. *When you imagine seeing the world as you desire it to be and are inspired as to its truth, it doesn't matter what anyone else thinks.* I don't care what it is; when you know what you want, you can make your desire so real, so natural that you will reach a feeling of certainty which no power in the world can stop. When that feeling is yours, drop it. Don't ask anyone if what you did was right or wrong; you did it and that's all that is necessary . . .

. . . I am saying, however, that you can be the man (or woman) you want to be, but not by simply wishing. *You must make the effort to look at the world mentally and see it reflect your fulfilled desire. And when it does you must remain in that state until you reach the inner conviction that what you are seeing, touching, tasting, smelling, and hearing is true, clothe yourself in the feeling of its reality—and explode!* Do that and you are pregnant. And what do you do after pregnancy? Nothing! You simply wait for its birth to appear in its own appointed hour. And it will! *When you least expect it your desire will objectify itself in the world for you to enjoy, whether it be health, wealth, or fame.* That's how God's law works.

Now, to the one who had this experience the other night, I know you are anxious to give it birth right away, but what is thirty years in this fabulous eternity? You were awake when it happened, and you will never lose its memory. Should you depart tonight to find yourself a young lady of twenty, you would only be fifty when you brought forth the Christ child. Then you would see the complete pattern fulfill itself in three and a half years* and enter a new age, which is the world of eternity. My dear, you are destined to know departure from this world of death and entrance into the world of eternal life as you move from darkness into light. But your reaction was natural.

It reminded me of a story I heard in New York City. This young girl came rushing into the subway, and standing in front of a gentleman she said: "Would you please let a pregnant lady have your seat?" Jumping up, terribly disturbed, the gentleman said: "When is the baby expected?" And she replied: "I don't know, it just happened." But this lady knows it will be thirty years, but what is thirty years when you have been called, you have been selected, you have been chosen. You are one of the elect!

---

* Neville is referencing a person passing into the afterworld and experiencing rebirth at age twenty, and then accomplishing his or her aim in three and a half years, which he calls the time span of Christ's ministry on earth. In his essay *Resurrection* (1966), Neville describes the fulfillment of Christ's three-and-a-half year ministry on earth with the Holy Spirit descending upon the individual in the form of a dove, bringing complete and final union with God. For further reference to this rebirth, see the lecture in this volume, "Election and Change of Consciousness." (E.g., "You do not die when men call you dead…")—MH

CHAPTER 20

"Remembering When"

Lecture, October 6, 1969

The objective reality of this world is solely produced by the human imagination, in which all things exist. Tonight I hope to show you how to subjectively appropriate that which already exists in you and turn it into an objective fact. Your life is nothing more than the out-picturing of your imaginal activity, for your imagination fulfills itself in what your life becomes.

The last year that Robert Frost (1874–1963) was with us, he was interviewed by *Life Magazine* and said: "Our founding fathers did not believe in the future, they believed it in." This is true.

Having broken with England, our founding fathers could have established their own royalty here by making one of them the king, thereby perpetuating a royal family. They could have chosen a form of dictatorship, but they agreed to imagine a form of government that had not been tried since the days of the Greeks. Democracy is the most difficult form of government in the world, yet our founding fathers agreed to believe it in. They knew it would take place, because they knew the power of belief—the power I hope to show you that you are, tonight.

To say: "I AM going to be rich," will not make it happen; you must believe riches in by claiming within yourself: "I AM rich." *You must believe in the present tense, because the active, creative power that you are, is God.* He is your awareness, and God alone acts and is. His name forever and ever is "I AM" therefore, he can't say: "I will be rich" or "I was rich" but "I AM rich!" Claim what you want to be aware of here and now, and although your reasonable mind denies it and your senses deny it, if you will assume it, with feeling, your inward activity, established and perpetuated, will objectify itself in the outside world, which is nothing more than your imaginal activity objectified.

To attempt to change the circumstances of your life before you change its imaginal activity is to labor in vain. This I know from experience. I had a friend who hated Roosevelt yet wanted him to change. Every morning while shaving my friend would tell Roosevelt off. He found great joy and satisfaction in this daily routine yet could not understand why Roosevelt stayed the same. *But I tell you, if you want someone to change, you must change your imaginal activity, for it is the one and only cause of your life.* And you can believe anything in if you will not accept the facts your senses dictate; for nothing is impossible to imagine and imagining—persisted in and believed—will create its own reality . . .

. . . We are told that God speaks to man in a dream and unveils himself in a vision. Now, vision is a waking dream like this room, while a dream occurs when you are not fully awake. A few years ago this vision was mine: I was taken in spirit into one of the early mansions on Fifth Avenue in New York City at the turn of the century. As I entered, I saw that three generations were present and I heard the eldest man telling the others of their grandfather's secret. *These are his words: "Grandfather used to say, while standing on an empty lot: 'I remember when this was an empty lot.' Then he would paint a word picture of what he wanted to build there. He saw it vividly in his mind's eye as he spoke, and in time it was established. He went through life in that manner, objectively realizing what he had first subjectively claimed."*

I tell you: everything in your outer world was first subjectively appropriated, I don't care what it is. Desire can be your empty lot where you may stand, remembering when that which you now have, was only a desire. *If I now say: "I remember when I lectured at the Woman's Club in Los Angeles" I am implying I am no longer there and am where I want to be. Remembering when you were poor, I have taken you out of poverty and placed you in comfort. I remember when you were sick, by taking you out of sickness and placing you in the state of health. I remember when you were unknown, implies you are now known. By changing my memory image of you, I can now remember when you, with all your fame and fortune, were unknown and broke. That was the secret of grandfather's success.*

This is what I learned in vision. Do not put this thought aside because it came to me in vision. In the 12th chapter of the Book of Numbers, it is said that God speaks to man through the medium of dreams and makes himself known through vision. If God makes himself known to you through vision, and speaks to you in dream, what is more important than to remember your dreams and visions? You can't compare the morning's paper or any book you may read, to your vision of the night, for that is an instruction from the depth of yourself.

God in you speaks to you in a dream, as he did to me when he took me on a trip in time to that beautifully staffed mansion at the turn of the century. As spirit, I was invisible to those present; but I heard more distinctly than they, and comprehended the words more graphically then they, because they had their millions; and who is going to tell one who already has millions how to get them. I entered their environment to hear their story in order to share it with those who will hear and believe my words and then try it.

This doesn't mean that, just because you heard my vision you are going to enjoy wealth; you must apply what you heard and *remember when. If you would say: "I remember when I couldn't afford to spend $400 a month for rent," you are implying you can well afford it now. The words: "I remember when it was a struggle to live on my monthly income," implies you have transcended that limitation. You can put yourself into any state by remembering when.* You can *remember when* your friend expressed her desire to be married. By *remembering when* she was single, you are persuading yourself that your friend is no longer in that state, as you have moved her from one state into another . . .

. . . Now, if imagination works this way, and it proves itself in the testing time and time again, what does it matter what the world thinks? It costs you nothing to try it, and what a change in life it will produce for you. Try it, for you will prove it in performance.

This may be in conflict with what you believe God to be. Maybe you still want him to be someone on the outside, so that there are two of you and not one. That's all right if you do, but I tell you: God became you that there would not be you and God. He became you, that you may become God. If God became you, his name must be in you, and it is; for if I ask you anything, you must first be aware of the question before you can respond, and your awareness is God.

You may not be aware of who you are, where you are, or what you are; but you do know that you are. Aware of what your senses and reason dictate, you may believe that you are limited, unwanted, ignored, and mistreated; and your world confirms your belief in your imaginal activity. And if you do not know that your awareness is causing this mistreatment, you will blame everyone but yourself; yet I tell you the only cause of the phenomena of life is an imaginal activity. There is no other cause.

If you believe in the horrors of the world as they are given to you in the paper and on television, your belief causes the horrors to continue. Believing the news of a shortage, you will buy what you do not need, blindly accepting the pressure to perpetuate an imaginal activity that keeps you frightened. All through Scripture you are told to let not your heart be troubled, be not afraid, and fear not. If fear could be eliminated, there would be no need for psychologists or psychiatrists. It's a bunch of nonsense, anyway. Every day this branch of medicine changes their concepts and they are always in conflict as to what a man's attitude towards life is.

I say to everyone: the whole vast world is now in your human imagination, and you can bring any desire out of it by *believing it into being.*

First, you must know what you want, then create an image that fulfills it. Would your friends know and talk about it? Imagine they are with you now, discussing your fulfilled desire. You could be at a cocktail or dinner party that is being given in your honor. Or maybe it's a little get-together over tea. Create a scene in your mind's eye and believe its reality in! That invisible state will produce the objective state you desire, for all objective reality is solely produced by imagination.

The clothes you are now wearing were first imagined. The chair in which you are seated, the room that surrounds you, there isn't a thing here that wasn't first imagined; so you can see that imagining creates reality. If you don't believe it, you are lost in a world of confusion.

There is no fiction. What is fiction today will be a fact tomorrow. A book written as a fictional story today comes out of the imagination of the one who wrote it and will become a fact in the tomorrows.

If you have a good memory or a good research system, you could find today's facts. Not every fact is recorded, because not every thought is written; yet every person imagines.

A man, feeling wrongfully imprisoned and desiring to get even, will disturb the world, because all things by a law divine in one another's being, mingle. You can't stop the force that comes from one who is imagining, because behind the mask he wears, you and he are one. Start now to become aware of what you are thinking, for as you think, you imagine. Only then can you steer a true course to your definite end. If you lose sight of that end, however, you can and will be moved by seeming others. But if you keep your mind centered in the awareness of dwelling in your destination, you cannot fail.

The end of your journey is where your journey begins. When you tell me what you want, do not try to tell me the means necessary to get it, because neither you nor I know them. Just tell me what you want that I may hear you tell me that you have it. If you try to tell me how your desire is going to be fulfilled, I must first rub that thought out before I can replace it with what you want to be. Man insists on talking about his problems. He seems to enjoy recounting them and cannot believe that all he needs to do is state his desire clearly. If you believe that imagination creates reality, you will never allow yourself to dwell on your problems, for you will realize that as you do you perpetuate them all the more.

So I tell you: the greatest thing you can do is to believe a thing into existence, just as our founding fathers did. They had no current example of democracy. It existed in Greece centuries ago, but failed because the Greeks changed their imaginal activity. We could do that too. Don't think for one second we have to continue as a democracy. We could be under dictatorship within twenty-four hours, for everything is possible. If you like democracy, you must be constantly watchful to keep its concepts alive within you. It's the most difficult form of government. A man can voice an opinion and stage a protest here, but in other forms of government he cannot. If you want to enjoy the freedom of a democracy, you must keep it alive by being aware of it.

Now, if you keep this law, you don't have to broadcast what you want; you simply assume that you have it, for ... although your reasonable mind and outer senses deny it ... if you persist in your assumption your desire will become your reality. There is no limit to your power of belief, and all things are possible to him who believes. Just imagine what an enormous power that is. You don't have to be nice, good, or wise, for anything is possible to you when you believe that what you are imagining is true. That is the way to success.

I believe any man who has been successful in his life's venture has lived as though he were successful. Living in that state, he can name those who aided him in achieving his success; and he may deny that he was always aware of success, but his awareness compelled the aid he received.

To believe your desire into being is to exercise the wonderful creative power that you are. We are told in the very first Psalm: "Blessed is the man who delights in the law of the Lord. In all that he does, he prospers." This law, as explained in the Sermon on the Mount, is psychological. "You have heard it said of old, thou shalt not commit adultery, but I say unto you, anyone who lusts after a woman has already committed the act of adultery with her in his heart." Here we discover that it is not enough to restrain the impulse on the outside. Adultery is committed the moment the desire is thought!

Knowing what you want, gear yourself towards it, for the act was committed in the wanting. Faith must now be added, for without faith it is impossible to please God. Can you imagine a state and feel that your imaginal act is now a fact? It costs you nothing to imagine; in fact you are imagining every moment in time, but not consciously. But, may I tell you: if you use your creative power by imagining a desire is already fulfilled, when you get it, the circumstances will seem so natural that it will be easy to deny your imagination had anything to do with it, and you could easily believe that it would have happened anyway. But if you do, you will have returned to sleep once again.

First of all, most of us do not even realize our own harvest when it confronts us. And if we do remember that we once imagined it, reason will tell us it would have happened anyway. Reason will remind you that you met a man (seemingly by accident) at a cocktail party who was interested in making money. When he heard your idea, he sent you to see his friend, and look what happened ... so really, it would have happened anyway. Then, of course, it is easy to ignore the law, but "Blessed is the man who delights in the law of the Lord. In all that he does he prospers."

Don't forget the law while you are living in the world of Caesar, and apply it wisely; but remember you are not justified by its use. Justification comes through faith. You must have faith in the incredible story that God promised to bring himself out of you, as you! This is God's promise to all, and all are asked to believe it.

It is not what you are, but what you trust God to do, that saves you. And to the degree that you trust God to save you, you will be saved. But he has given us a psychological law to cushion the inevitable blows of life. The law is simple: "As you sow, so shall you reap." It is the law of like begets like. As you imagine, so shall your life become. Knowing what you want, assume the feeling that would be yours if you had it. Persist in that feeling, and in a way you do not know and could not devise, your desire will become a fact. Grandfather made his fortune by standing on an empty lot and saying to himself: "I remember when this was an empty lot." Then he would paint a beautiful word picture of the structure he desired there. This is a wonderful technique. You can remember when you were unknown, penniless, and ill, or a failure. Remembering when you were, implies you are no longer that, and your power is in its implication.

Use the law and it will take you from success to success, as you conceive success to be. As far as I am concerned, success is to fulfill the promise, and you cannot do that through the law. The promise is fulfilled through faith. Are you holding true to the faith? Examine yourself to see if you are. I have told you an eternal story. Believe it, but do not change it. The story is this: God became you that you may become God. Use the law to cushion the blows while God keeps his promise; and then one day, when your journey is over, you will say: "Into thy hands I commit my spirit. Thou hast redeemed me, O Lord, faithful God." That's the cry on the cross. Commit your spirit to your imaginal act, relax and fall asleep knowing its redemption is assured. Then when you least expect it, God will prove to you that he has redeemed you by awakening in you, as you. Then you will be born, not of blood or of the will of the flesh, or of the will of man, but of God.

CHAPTER 21

"Even the Wicked"

Lecture, May 5, 1972*

We have only to enlarge our conception of causality to excuse everything and forgive all. Now, let me just state one little thought from Scripture first before we unfold it. As we are told in the 25th chapter of Genesis, "In your limbs lie nations twain, rival races from their birth; one the mastery will gain, the younger o'er the elder reign." The first one is the sense man. I'm now looking at this room and all within it and that is the sense man. My normal apprehension of corporeal objects just like this room and the contents, I call sense perceived. That which is not present, and yet I perceive it, I call that imag-

* This is one of Neville's final lectures, delivered about five months before his death on October 1, 1972. It is transcribed in full for the first time in this collection.—MH

ination. That is destined to rule. That is the second man, the Lord from heaven.

The first man is of the Earth, a man of dust. The second is from heaven. So here we are in this world, and this is the world of this dual state within every child born of woman. And so we have the physical man, the man of dust, and then we have the spiritual man, the man of imagination. That is the immortal man. When I see this picture of the duality of man and how all things are created by this hidden man, I forgive everything in this world that the physical man does, *for the physical man is only a state.* One being is playing all the parts. *The part played by the thief is the same being playing the part of the judge who judges the thief.* The part who is the murderer and the murdered, he's a part but the being within, he's one.

Now, let me explain it first in the beginning with a simple story. About eight years ago, I was in New York for a month, and two of my brothers, Victor and Lawrence, came up and spent two weeks with me in New York City. They're checked into the same hotel. They wanted to see everything they could within two weeks, and I bought them fourteen shows. And sometimes they went even to an afternoon show. They wanted to see everything in the crowded two weeks. But the one thing my brother, Lawrence, wanted to see was the new presentation of *Aida*.

Well, the papers say it was sold out from the very moment that it was announced. Same music naturally, the same score, but new scenery. Something new about it. Now, this captured the imagination of all opera lovers and they all wanted to see *Aida*. The one thing he wanted to see was *Aida* but the papers had huge big ads, not one seat is available. Come down and buy a seat for the other shows and this was the old opera house around 40th Street and Broadway. It ran from Broadway through 7th Avenue, the old Metropolitan. So, this morning we set out and I said, "It doesn't really matter, let us go. We have to go down and have lunch anyway. We will go and just see."

We got there and these huge big signs on the outside: "No seats for *Aida* available," and they were plastered all over the Metropolitan. I went in and there were three lines leading towards the three windows selling tickets for the entire season, and there was no seat for *Aida*. I got into the first line. It was a very long line then I saw the third line from me moving more rapidly than the first and the second, so I moved over to that line. Then we all move rapidly forward. As we got to the window, and seemingly no hope of getting tickets, but before I left my hotel room, I simply assumed that I had the tickets for my two brothers. I didn't want to go. They wanted to see it, so I assumed that I gave them the tickets.

I got into this line. We move rapidly towards the window. As we got there to the window, a tall blonde man, he must have been about six-foot-four, stretched his hand up over my head and diverted the ticket seller as he asked a question while one in front of me is buying seats, not for *Aida* because that's completely sold out, he is buying two other seats for some other opera. Then he departed after he diverted the man's attention. This man pushed on some bills under the window and then as the teller looked at the money—and this man is at the door now, the tall, tall blonde fellow—and he's given this man the ticket and then suddenly he said, "For he only gave me $3. He should have given me,"—and he mentioned the money he should have given me. At that, he was bewildered, the teller was bewildered. I turned around and I screamed at that tall blond. I said, "Sir!" I screamed so loudly he couldn't stop, but the attendant, he turned around, I said, "Come back here. You're wanted." He came back like a little child being led by the nose. He came back and he said, "What's wrong?" And the man said, "This is all that he gave me. Two $1 bills." Said, "Oh no, he didn't. He gave you two 10s." Then I said, "No, you didn't. I was standing right here. I saw what you did. You gave him two $1 bills. That's all that you gave him."

The man was flabbergasted. He was so completely dumbfounded, he didn't know what to do. I said, "I am standing here. I saw exactly what was done." Then he opened up his purse and here was a stack of 1s and he had a $20 bill and two 10s. He said to the man, "Say when you discover your mistake that I gave you two 10s," and the man said to him, "At the end of the season." And with that, it was closed, and the man then took out the money and paid for the tickets and took back his two 1s.

Then I said to him, "I want two seats for *Aida* tonight and I want them in the horseshoe circle. I want them center." He said, "Yes, sir," and he took from what is called the VIP. They always keep a few out. Though the house is sold out, they always keep a few seats for those who are coming called the very important people. I am certainly not a very important person, but I saved him from the loss of $20 and he quickly took the two seats out and said to me, "$20." I gave him the $20, and gave the two seats to my brothers.

Now, a state called a thief. These two men have chosen to be thieves in their world. They're con men. It's perfectly all right. God made everything for its purpose and even the are wicked for the time of trouble. Read that in the 16th chapter, the fourth verse of Proverbs. "He made everything for its purpose, even the wicked, for the day of trouble." For the day of trouble may not be a war. I was troubled how to get these tickets. That's a moment of trouble and I simply assumed that I had them. I simply played my part in my imagination before I left my hotel room that my brothers are going to see this show this night of *Aida*, the new presentation of *Aida*.

They two, who have already given themselves over to the state of a thief, they had to actually come right into the line. I took the first line then I move over to the third line because I saw it moving more rapidly, so he comes over to the third line and pays his part beautifully. If he had not done what he did, I would not have received those tickets because I am not a very important person; but the man looked me in the eyes and thought here was an honest man. As far as he is concerned, I am an honest man who saved him from losing $20. And so he quickly took out the two seats. I paid for them— naturally he didn't give them to me. I was willing to pay for my seats, but you couldn't buy them. All over the place, "sold out, sold out, sold out," all over the Metropolitan Opera. You could paste it on the wall; I mean a huge big ad in the paper "Aida is sold out." And I went that day and got those seats right in the circle in center row for my two brothers because one man played his part beautifully. He had given himself over to a con man. He finds it easy to make a living being a con man. There are those who are pickpockets. There are schools to teach people to be pickpockets. Do you know that? They come right out of the school and go into a profession. All right, that's their part. They play that part.

Now, you play your part beautifully, and one of them can be instrumental in getting you what you want in this world. So I wanted two seats for *Aida*. Were it not for a con man in that world, I would not have had those two seats.

So he comes into the line where I was in the line, he comes forward, and just as I got to the ticket window, he puts his hand over my head to divert the man's attention. And the one in front of me who is buying two seats, not for *Aida* because you can't get them, he is buying two seats for something else. And he puts out two dollar bills instead of two 10s, and then this man starts and I turn around as though I was inspired, and with my full voice I said, "Sir, come back here!" He had to come back. So he came on back just like a little child and stood next to me, and he looked down at me. He wouldn't dare budge. Well, I said, "You didn't give him anything more than what he is showing you now. You've given him exactly what he's showing you," because I was fair and I stood next to you. He was helpless. He couldn't hit me. He was many inches my height. I was five-eleven and he may be about six-five or more. A strong strapping blond but he was impotent in my presence when I called him back.

He only played the part, so should I not forgive him? There are infinite states in this world and all you have to do is forget states. You play your part in every state necessary to make your part come to fulfillment will be present at the moment that you need it. And so we went out for lunch, and my brothers, Lawrence and Victor, they had their tickets and that evening, they went to see *Aida*.

So in your limbs lie nations twain. They are rival races from their birth, one the mastery shall gain, the younger over the elder reign. And the younger is the second and the second man is the man from heaven, and that man is your own wonderful human imagination who is God. And there is no other God. That is the Lord from heaven and the outer man that clothes him, he is under compulsion to fulfill the commands of that inner man. But everyone is falling into states, infinite states; to understand this world you must think in terms of states. He has made everything for its purpose, even the wicked for the day of trouble.

And so use everything, but you don't have to think of which one will do it, forget it, who will play the part. I never saw that man before. Never saw his partner in their little crime before. That was their choice in life. There are those who have chosen to be pickpockets for the rest of their lives, so if they are caught in the act, all right, that's part of the game. They've chosen that part to play. Now, those who have chosen their part to play like Mr. Hoover who just departed this world. He chose that part and there are others who chose other parts.

Either wisely or unwisely, we fall into these things; but when the inner man begins to awake, he selects his part wisely. It's entirely up to us, so I tell you, everything in this world that you want to be, you can be if you will know that there are only states. You move into the state because the occupant of the state does not differ from the occupant of any other state. The one who played the part that day of the con man to get two tickets for $2 instead of $20, and go on the street and sell them for $15 and make himself a quick few bucks.

The same occupant is God. God is playing all the parts, so all we have to do is simply to expand a little bit our conception of causality to actually excuse everything and forgive everyone in this world. I forgave him because he actually was instrumental in getting me the two seats for my brothers. Were he not playing that part at that moment, I would not have had the seats. But before I left my hotel room, I simply assumed that my brothers had their seats, and they were going to see *Aida*, and they came off thrilled beyond measure, so we went down at seemingly no hope.

I wasn't concerned about any hope. There were three long, long lines. After all you're selling out just for the show of the night. You're selling for the afternoon show, you're selling for the evening show, and for the entire season, and buy a month in advance, two months in advance. They're all there and so here are the lines and your three lines and three windows open. And what caused me to move to that moving window? The father in me. He knew which one is going to play what part because they're all in states and myself is fully aware of all the states in the world. And if you can play a part to aid me in the fulfillment of my dream, you will play it.

If I need a thief, there must be a thief somewhere. He was a thief and he played the part, better part in my getting the ticket than if he were an honest man. If he came up and played the part of an honest man, then the man would have said to me, he wouldn't know me, I'm not an important person, and so we have no tickets. Go into signs, "No tickets available." It's a sellout but it was not a sellout and a thief made it possible for me to get my two tickets.

So when you see this, you forgive every being in the world, *everyone*. They're all playing their part, so don't condemn anyone because everyone will be instrumental in fulfilling your dream if you know this law. It's all infinite states but remember you are awakening to the reality of the second man. In this room, my simple apprehension of corporeal objects, the things on the wall, your hair, the chair, the house, this thing for a wedding tomorrow, all this preparation for a wedding. All this is to my sense man reality and I think of something entirely different, and that is called only imagination, and that is the second man.

Now, what do I want in place of what my senses are telling me? Let me now enter into that state and live it as though it were true and move forward in that state. Now, let me show you the difference now because we started with that statement from the 25th chapter of the book of Genesis.

An idea that is only an idea produces nothing and does nothing. It must be felt, actually felt, so that it awakens within oneself certain sensations, certain local actions, in order to be effective. What would the feeling be like if it were true? Dwell upon that until the feeling awakes within you these sensations, for imagination is spiritual sensation. That is the creative being in you. It's not just to entertain an idea; not idea. The idea must produce in you this feeling which is a sensation, but it must be a *feeling*. What would the feeling we like if it were true? You dwell upon that until you catch that feeling.

As Churchill said, that the mood determines the fortunes of people rather than the fortunes the mood; the mood precedes the fortune. So what would you want in this world of contemplating? What would the feeling be like if you had it? What would it be like if it were true? That is the story of Scripture. If I could only feel that I am already the man that I want to be, that I'm already the woman that I want to be, and feeling, then it's not only an idea, which as an idea without feelings will produce nothing, now, it has everything because in this story, you say to the second man, "Come close, my son, that I may feel you."

The secret is in the feeling. So he's always out. He is the first man covered with fear, the outer man, and Jacob is the inner man, the man of imagination who is hairless. It isn't two little boys. These are only symbols. It's all in man, so come close my son that I may feel you. So he comes close and deceives his father through feeling, so the father feels and he feels them just to be externally real. *You can do it. There is no flower in your hand but you can feel the soft velvet feeling of a rose. You can smell a rose though it's not physically present. Try it. Try all these things with the inner man and when you can actually feel it so that you raise your imagination to the point of sensation, to vision, then the whole thing is done.*

It's done in a way you do not know it's going to happen. If it takes a thief to aid you, then you forgive the thief. Should I not forgive that man who tried to rob that teller of $20 when he did for me what no one else could do? I could go to all the brokers in New York City and they couldn't get me two seats. I could go to anyone and they couldn't get me two seats for my two brothers, and I wanted them to have the joy of seeing the new presentation of *Aida*, so I went myself prepared in my imagination that I had two seats. And it took a thief to be instrumental in getting me the seats. Should I not forgive him for the part he played?

He went to the door, this tall, giant of a man. He looked back at me but he wouldn't have the courage to come up and slap me. *There was something in me that dwarfed him in his own mind's eye, so in spite of his height and his bigness and his strength, he couldn't dare strike me for I was speaking from a different level of consciousness altogether, so I didn't condemn him.* He played the part he had to play and by playing it, I got the seats. *So all we have to do is simply to widen, just widen a little bit, our conception of causality to actually forgive all in the world, to excuse everything in the world.*

They're playing their part. So tonight you want a bigger job, you want more money in this world, you want—and you name it. Well, it may be a thief who is going to aid you into getting without knowing he is doing it. Don't judge him. Don't condemn him. Just simply—you go forward knowing that I have ways and means that the physical man knows not of. My ways, the inner man's ways are past finding out, and you simply go forward in the assumption that you have already achieved what now is only a wish as far as the world is concerned, but you enter into the wish as though the wish is already fulfilled.

So what would the feeling be like? "Come near, my son, that I may feel you," and so he comes close. He said, "Come nearer, my son." Then he said to him, "You know, your voice is the voice of Jacob, but your hands, your neck, and your scent, you have the feel of my son Esau." Esau is the outer world, so he gives emphasis to feeling. It transcends the voice. The voice was Jacob's but the feeling, that touch was that of an external world. He could feel the external world. It was a self-deception. He saved himself into believing that what he desired, he had.

It's not two little boys born of woman. All this is parable. *The whole story of the Bible is all parabolic*, telling stories that unless you have the depth to understand it, well then you'll never really; but me I say you will, eventually you will, and you certainly do understand it now. So tonight, is a practical night. Do you know this night what you want, really what you want? Well, if you do, do the same thing I did in getting the two seats.

Do what I did when I was locked out completely from marrying the girl I wanted to marry. I simply assumed that she slept here, I slept here, and I went sound asleep, and in one week, my wife did an act which certainly I must forgive in the eyes of the world. She is condemned for taking what she did not pay for, and yet because of that act, I got my freedom. Then who is the culprit? Am I not? If there's any culprit, I am. If there's any culprit in this world, it is God.

There is nothing but God. God is doing all in this world. He created everything in this world, and so I fit in me, he is the second man, and the second man is my imagination, and that is God, for men is all imagination and God is man and exists in us, and we in him. The eternal body of man is the imagination and that is God himself. Well, if I in my imagination slept as though I am happily married to a girl that the laws of New York State said I could never get because of my entanglement with my first wife, and in one week she performed an act which was judged harshly by society and yet she was the instrument of my getting my freedom to marry the girl who now is the mother of my daughter.

How can I blame her to perform that act? She was in a state—and who did it? I did it. I did it by simply assuming that I was free and happily married to a girl that the state of New York said I could never marry because of these ancient laws that restricted my desire to get freedom in that state. So you'll forgive everyone in this world to all playing their parts. In my own case, I have seen thieves, I have seen all kinds of people play their part; they were instruments in the fulfillment of my desire, so how can I ever condemn all? The last cry on the cross, "Father, forgive them. They know not what they do. Forgive them."

The whole vast world is playing until he awakes in that body. He is playing the part and he plays it automatically, unwittingly, for one who was awake, who knows exactly what he's doing, and so they all play their parts, for God in everyone is the same God. There aren't two gods. There's only one God—and that God is your own wonderful human imagination. When you say *I am*, that's God.

So tonight, you just completely boldly declare that you are the man, you are the woman that you want to be, and walk in that assumption as though it were true and then let all these sleeping states play their part. Now, I tell you, in spite of what they appear to be, they are sound, sound asleep. They do not know. He thought he knew what he did. He came right in into my line and played his part. I could have remained on the first line and waited and waited and waited, and no one would have played their part there. I moved over to the moving line and here he comes, and so how could I ever condemn him? How could I ever, in any way, feel other than thankful?

I would say to him, "Thank you because you played the part you had to play," like a play, so someone comes in on the play. The curtain goes up and here comes the monster, and he plays it beautifully. And the audience hisses and condemns him. If there's any condemnation of the part, where is the author? Send for the author for he wrote the part, and the author, if there's any praise, give it to the author. Any condemnation, give it to the author.

I know I've played a part, a second part, on a play on Broadway. And if I didn't get a hiss when I came on, if they didn't hiss me, I felt I wasn't doing well. But I would say 99 percent of the time as I came on and started to play my part, the audience hissed. Then I knew I was really on my toes. I was playing the part well because I was a cad in that part and they couldn't restrain themselves especially with the matinees when they had children there. Lots of ladies and children, and they could not restrain their emotion and they were hissing for then I knew, "Neville you're getting over all right."

So I was thrilled with their hissing because I was playing only what was written for me to play. So in this wonderful world of ours, we are infinite states, and everyone is in a state, but the one being in one state is the being in all states. There's only one player. God only acts and is in existing beings or name. He is in all the states and His name in all states is *I am*. So someone chooses the part and he wants to be, well, a thief. He finds it easier. He thinks, "I'm getting up, going to work, and punching a clock, and punching it out." He feels it's better for him to live that life. All right. So he has chosen that part, if he does it deliberately, for he might have fallen into it through habit of others and then it's unwittingly. All right. But he will also pay the price.

That is the thing he has to consider. He will pay the price because the part has a price with it; but in spite of that, he can be used in the fulfillment of your dreams. Now, many of you who have had, from your letters, dreams of death recently. May I tell you, it's a healthy, healthy sign. *Dreams are egocentric. You cannot grow and not outgrow in this world. To outgrow is to die. You die to one state and you move into another state.*

So anyone dreaming of death, many of you have dreamt of my death numberless times, as Paul said, "I die daily." Every day, he grows. If he did not die every day well then he didn't grow that day. So death, when you see yourself buried or you see yourself in a coffin or you see these things in your dream, it's only a beautiful symbol of your growth. You are growing, that's why you see yourself buried, why you see yourself in a tomb. It's simply an expansion of consciousness, so you die to one state of consciousness as you enter a greater state of consciousness.

So when people see themselves dying or others say, "you're dead," it has nothing to do with a little physical body because you don't die anyway, not really for nothing dies. It's always an expansion and expansion and expansion, so when you do see yourself being buried, give praise. You have died to your former beliefs and these arcane concepts that you entertain which only enslaved you. Right now, someone introduces you to a new idea and you toy with the idea of accepting it, but you resist it for a while. Then suddenly, you see your body being entombed. It means it's gotten hold of you. These new ideas that will call you to an expansion of yourself, and so the old man dies that the new man may live.

A seed must fall into the ground and die before it can be made alive. If it does not fall into the ground and die then it cannot bring forth fruit. It simply remains what it was before. So if it dies, it bears much fruit. So don't be afraid of any vision of death. *Death is the most glorious symbol in the mysteries of the expansion of consciousness.* Man is expanding and expanding and expanding in this world, and one day, his wonderful imagination will awaken, and that is God.

Then he sees a whole vast world as sleepers, all sleepers, and how can you condemn the sleeper? So he played his part. He played it beautifully. I can see all these things in my world where people play some many marvelous parts, and they were sound asleep, and they thought they were so alert, going to get the better of me, and their attempts to get the better were exactly what I needed to move on. Just move on. They had no idea they're playing their part beautifully. *So I forgive all the thieves that came into my world, even those who took, actually took from my pocket by not giving me what the contract called for; I thank them because it simply allowed me to become all the more secure upon my own feet, and not think for one second that I depended upon them or for anyone else in this world, so let them go their way.*

They're all sound, sound asleep playing their parts. But this thing that happened, I would say about seven, eight years ago, It was so forceful in my mind. My brothers thought that I was very courageous with this giant over my head to do what I did. It wasn't any courage. At that moment, I saw what he did. And when I said to him, "You didn't do it at all. I saw what you did. You stopped $2 there and there they are. You didn't give him any $10 bills." He opened up his purse and I saw all these 1s, oodles of 1s and then a 20, and a couple of 10s at the side. And then he pulled out the 10s and gave them and took his two 1s back. And then he went back to the door with the other partner of his and looked at me as though he could have killed me but he didn't have the guts to hit me. He couldn't.

If I were that big, he could have struck me, because I was speaking on an entirely different level, and on that level when I knew I was going to get my seats, that's all that concerned me. Here comes the two seats and the man said, "Yes, sir." He treated me as though I stood before him as the president and he thought, "Now, here is an honest man who saved me $20." I'm only playing the part. I only wanted two seats that night because that's all that my brothers could give because I had all these seats brought for them. All the shows for Broadway at the time within two weeks and every night after night and matinees and everything else. Got it right up to their heads in shows.

So I'm telling you, if you know of this dual being within you, *in your limbs lie nations twain, rival races from their birth; one the mastery will gain, the younger over the elder reign.* Now, see that that younger one actually reigns and the younger one is your imagination. The older one is your sense man. The facts, these are the facts of life. What does my bank account—and I owe more than the bank account—have in it now? Well, now that is Esau's judgment.

Now, Jacob puts in 50 times what is there now. In my mind's eye, I deposited 50 times more than is there. How it's going to happen, I don't know. I don't know any more than I knew that day when I started all for the Metropolitan Opera, how I'm going to buy seats when the papers tell me you can't buy a seat. Huge big ad, "Save your time and don't come" or "Other seats are available but not for *Aida*." I go down only for *Aida* and I get them because of a seeming thief played by the part of God. For God plays all the parts in the world. There is nothing but God, and say *I am*—that's God.

That is the Lord Jesus within you. That is your immortal being that cannot die. He cannot die. That is your eternal self when you say, *I am. Imagination is not some vague essence. It is a body, a reality, an infinite body that is so perfect when it's awakened that in its presence everything is made perfect.* But while it is awakening, it exercises that power and draws into its world everyone that can play their part for its fulfillment of its dream.

So here I hope you heard it clearly. I hope I made it as clear as I can because tonight should be a very practical night that you will go out knowing who you are. You're a dual being. But the first man is of the dust, and to dust, he returns. That is the man of Earth. The second man is the Lord from heaven and He cannot die. That's your own wonderful human imagination. It cannot die but it keeps. It sleeps embodied in this tomb and one day, it will awaken. As I've told you in the past, the symbolism of Scripture will surround you. It's perfect. It is true. Everything told to you in Scripture as to his birth, you are going to experience, and then your imagination awakens. And you'd trust no one but it, only this being within you do you really worship. Let them give all the medals and all the honors to this, that, and the other to the little earthly man. It doesn't interest you.

Chariot of Fire:
The Ideas of Neville Goddard

Lecture by Mitch Horowitz,
June 28, 2013[*]

Some of you know my work, my book *Occult America,* and things that I've done related to that. *Occult
America* is a history of supernatural religious movements in our country. A few of you who know my
work are aware that I feel strongly that occult, esoteric, and metaphysical movements have touched
this country very deeply. I write about these move-

---

[*] This was my first public talk on Neville, delivered at the now-
defunct arts space Observatory in Gowanus, Brooklyn. Observatory
launched many ideas, writers, and cultural movements. This talk
appears here for the first time in print.—MH

ments not only as a historian who is passionately interested in how the paranormal, occult, and supernatural have influenced our religion, our economy, our psychology, and our views of ourselves; but I also write about these things as a participant, as a kind of a believing historian. I do not view occult thought movements strictly as historical phenomena, which may reveal aspects of human nature; that's true enough, but I think that within the folds of such movements there exist actual ideas for human transformation.

I don't believe in looking into philosophies simply in order to place them in museum cases and to label them. Rather, I think we need practical philosophies that contribute to real-life transformation in the here and now. In my study of different occult and mystical systems, some of which I wrote about in *Occult America* and some of which I'm writing about in my next book *One Simple Idea*, I must tell you the most impactful, elegant, simplest, and dramatically powerful figure I have come across is Neville Goddard.

He was born to an Anglican family on the island of Barbados in 1905. It was a family of ten children, nine boys and one girl. Neville came here to New York City to study theater in 1922. He had some success and also fell into a variety of mystical and occult philosophies. Neville eventually came to feel that he had discovered the master key to existence. Up to this point in my experiments, I conclude: he may have been right.

You can determine that for yourself, because I'm going to start off this presentation by giving you his system. I am also going to provide some history: where he came from, who his teachers were, what his ideas grew out of, who he has influenced, and why he proved vastly ahead of his time. Some of the methods and ideas that Neville experimented with are being heard about today through unsensational-ized discussions of developments in quantum phys-ics and neurobiology.

I will also consider the possible identity of the hidden spiritual master named Abdullah who Nev-ille said was his teacher in New York City. Are there spiritual masters, masters of wisdom in the world? Are there beings who can provide help to us when we sincerely desire it? Is that a real possibility or is that just fantasy? I think it's a possibility. It may have played out in his existence.

But we're really here to talk about the practical side of his philosophy. There are many interesting figures who I reference in this talk—dramatic figures whose lives spanned the globe. But we're talking about Neville *because of the usefulness of his ideas* and I want to start with that.

Mind as God

Neville believed very simply in the principle that your imagination is God, the human imagination is God, and that Scripture and all the stories from Scripture, both Old Testament and New Testament, have absolutely no basis in historical reality. The entire book is a metaphor, a blueprint for the individual's personal development. In particular, the New Testament tells the story of God symbolically, of God descending into human form, of humanity becoming asleep to its own divine essence or Christ essence, and believing itself to live within a coarse, limited world of material parameters, of then being crucified and experiencing the agony of his forgetfulness. Christ yells out in the across, "My God, my God, why has thou forsaken me?" The individual is then resurrected into the realization of his or her divine potentiality, which is the birthright of every individual.

Neville maintained, through his reading of Scripture, his personal probing as a philosopher, and his experiments as an individual, that there is no God outside of the creative powers of the imagination; and that those who wrote Scripture never intended to communicate that there was a God outside of the individual's imagination. The creative force within us—which thinks, plans, pictures, ponders, and falls in and out of emotive states—is symbolically represented in Scripture as God.

Neville maintained that your thoughts, your mental pictures, and your emotive states create your concrete reality—and do at every moment of existence. We are oblivious and asleep to this fact. We live in these coarse shells, we suffer, we cry, we have fleeting joys, we leave these forms. We go through life in a state of slumber without ever knowing that each one of us is a physical form in which creation is experiencing itself. We eventually come to the realization through our causative minds we can experience the powers written about in symbolically in the New Testament and embodied as the story of Christ resurrected.

I want to say to you that Neville meant all of this in the most radical and literal sense. There was nothing inexact or qualified in what he said. He took a radical stand and he continually put up a challenge to his audiences: *try it.* Try it tonight and if it doesn't work, discard me, discard my philosophy, prove me a liar. He sold nothing. He published a handful of books, most of which are now public domain. He gave lectures Grateful Dead-style where he allowed everybody to tape record them and distribute them freely, which is why his talks are now all over the Internet. There's nothing to join. There's nothing to buy. There's no copyright holder. There's just this man and his ideas.

Three-Step Miracle

Neville's outlook can be reduced to a three-part formula, which is incredibly simple, but also requires commitment.

First, every creative act begins with an absolute, passionate desire. It sounds so easy, doesn't it? We walk around all day long with desires; I want this, I want that, I want money, I want relationships, I want this person to pay attention to me, I want this attainment. But look again. We often have superficial understandings of our desires and we're dishonest about our desires.

We're dishonest about our desires because we don't want to say to ourselves, in our innermost thoughts, *what we really want*. Sometimes we're repulsed by our desires, and that's the truth. We live in a society that's filled with so much personal license and freedom on the surface, of course, but we often don't want to acknowledge things to ourselves that maybe we believe aren't attractive.

I want to tell a personal story and I want to be very personal with you because I'm talking to you about a man and a philosophy that is enormously challenging and practical, if you really take it seriously. I have no right to be standing here talking to you unless I tell you about some of my own experiences. I want to tell you about one of my personal experiences as it relates to this first point: *desire.* Years ago, I knew a woman who was a psychic. A nationally known person, somebody I assume some of you have heard of, not household name maybe, but well known. I thought she had a genuine psychical gift. I thought she had something.

Yet I didn't like the way she led her life because I thought, personally, that she could be a violent person—not physically violent but emotionally; she would manipulate people around her, bully people, push people around. I didn't really like her but I did feel that she had a true gift. One night I was talking to her. We were on a parking lot somewhere having conversation, and she stopped. She said to me, "You know what you want? You want power. But your problem is that you have an overdeveloped super-ego." As soon as I heard this I wanted to push it away. And I spent years pushing it away. Years pushing it away because I thought to myself, "Well, I don't want power like you. I don't want power to push people around, to bully people, to be violent towards people. I don't want that, no." So I recoiled from what she said. But it haunted me. It haunted me. I could never get away from it.

You don't know really what haunts you until you confront something in yourself, or maybe something that a sensitive person says to you, which leaves the terrible impression that they might just may be speaking the truth. So when Neville talks about desire, he's not talking about something superficial that we keep telling ourselves day after day. He really wants you to get down into the guts of things, where you might want something that makes you very uncomfortable. There are ways we don't like to see ourselves. But Neville maintains that desire is the voice of the God within you; and to walk away from it is to walk away from the potential greatness within yourself. Desire is the language of God. Neville means this in the most literal sense.

The second step is physical immobility. This is the part where you actually do something. You enter a physically immobile state. Choose the time of day when you like to meditate, whether it's early morning, whether it's late at night. The time of day Neville chose was 3:00 p.m. He would finish lunch, settle into an easy chair, and go into a drowsy state. Now, this is very important because we think of meditation typically as a state of exquisite awareness. We don't think of meditation as drowsiness. People use these terms in different ways. Neville believed—and as I will talk about this later in this presentation—that the mind is uniquely powerful and suggestible in its drowsy state, hovering just before sleep, but not yet crossing into sleep. It is a controlled reverie. Or a cognizant dream state. Sleep researchers call this hypnagogia. You enter it twice daily: at night when you're drifting off and in the morning when you're coming to (this is sometimes called hypnopompia).

Our minds are exquisitely sensitive at such times. People who suffer from depression or grief describe their early morning hours as the most difficult time of day. The reason for that, I'm convinced, is that it is a time when our rational defenses are down. We're functioning almost entirely from emotion. We are conscious but we are also in this very subtle, fine state between sleep and wakefulness, and our rational defenses are slackened. Let me tell you something vital—and I can attest to this from personal experience. If you are trying to solve a personal problem, do not do it at 5:00 in the morning. Do not.

Your rational defenses are down when you need them most.

When you need your intellect, whether you're solving a financial problem, whether you're going through a relationship problem, whatever it is, do not use the time of day when it is at its lowest ebb. At 5 a.m. your mind isn't fully working. Your emotions are working. It is a tough, tough time to deal with problems. But it is a very unique time to deal with desires—and for the same reason. When your rational defenses are down, your mind can go in remarkable directions.

I'm going to talk later about developments in psychical research, where there are some extraordinary findings under rigorous clinical conditions, in which people are induced into this hypnagogic state, the state between sleep and wakefulness, and the mind can evince remarkable abilities.

So, Neville said to enter this state of physical immobility. You can most easily do it just before you go to sleep at night. He didn't say do it when you wake up in the morning but I think you can extrapolate that that works, too. You can also do it when you're meditating. You can do it whenever you want. It takes only a few minutes, but go into a very relaxed bodily state or just let yourself be taken into it naturally when you go to bed at night.

And now *the third step*: form a very clear, simple mental scene that would naturally occur following the fulfillment of your desire. Keep it very simple. Run it through your head as long as it feels natural.

A woman attended one of Neville's lectures in Los Angeles and told him simply that she wanted to be married. He told her to enact the mental feeling of a wedding band on her finger. Just that. Keep it very simple. Mentally feel the weight and pressure of the ring on your finger. Maybe feel yourself spinning it around on your finger. Maybe there's something you want from an individual. Select an act that seems simple. Just a handshake, perhaps. Something that communicates that you received something—recognition, a promotion, a congratulation.

You must picture yourself *within* the scene. You must see from within the scene. Don't see yourself doing something as though you're watching it on a screen. Neville was adamant about this. He would say, "If I want to imagine myself climbing a ladder, I don't *see* myself climbing a ladder. *I climb*." You must feel hands on the ladder. Feel your weight was you step up each rung. You are not watching the scene—you are in it.

Whatever it is, find one simple, clear, persuasive, physical action that would communicate the attainment of your goal, and think from that end, think from the end of the goal fulfilled. Run this through your mind as long as it feels natural.

Neville would always say, "When you open your eyes, you'll be back here in the coarse world that you might not want to be in, but if you persist in this, your assumption will harden into fact." You may wake up, come out of your physical immobility, and discover that the world remains exactly as it was. If you want to be in Paris and you open your eyes in New York, you may be disappointed. Keep doing it and extraordinary events will unfold to secure precisely what you have pictured in your mind. Persistence is key.

Using the Emotions

Now, I want to emphasize one aspect of Neville's philosophy, which I feel that he could have gone further in explaining, and that is the necessity of your visual scene being accompanied by the attendant emotional state. We often make the mistake in the positive-mind movement of equating thought with emotions. They are different things. I have a physical existence. I have intellectual existence. I have an emotional existence. Part of why you may feel torn apart when approaching mind causation is that all of these aspects of your existence—the physical, the mental, and the emotional—are going their own way, running on separate tracks. You may vow not to eat, and you may mean it, but the body wants to eat—and next thing you know the body is in control. You may vow not to get angry—but the emotions take over and you fly into rage. You may think, "I am going to use my intellect and not my passions"—but the passions rule your action. These three forces, body, mind, and intellect, have their own lives—and intellect is the weakest among them. Otherwise we

wouldn't struggle with addictions or violent out-
bursts or impulsive actions. But we find that we are
pieces.

This presents a challenge. Because when you
enact your mental scene of fulfillment, you also
must attain the emotive state that you would feel in
your fulfillment. When you approach this teaching
you benefit from being a kind of actor or thespian,
as Neville was early in his career. Method Acting is a
good exercise for enacting this method. Read Stan-
islavski's *An Actor Prepares*. Anybody who's been
trained in Method Acting often learns to use a kind
of inner monologue to get themselves into an emotional state. That's a good exercise. You must get the
emotions in play.

Let's say you want a promotion at work. You could
picture your boss saying to you, "Congratulations—
well done!" You must try to feel the emotions that
you would feel in that state. Hypnagogia can also help
with this because, as noted, the rational defenses are
lowered and the mind is more suggestible.

To review Neville's formula: 1) Identify an intense
and sincere desire. 2) Enter a state of physical immobility, i.e., the drowsy hypnagogic state. 3) Gently run
a scene through your mind that would occur if your
wish was fulfilled. Let it be an emotional experience.

How It Happened

I want to tell another personal story. Neville always challenged his listeners, "Test it. Test it. What do you most desire right now? Go home this night and test it. Prove me wrong," he would say. I decided to test him and I want to give you the example. It is recent to this talk, explicit, and absolutely real.

In addition to being a writer, I'm a publisher. I'm the editor-in-chief of a division of Penguin that publishes New Age and metaphysical books. After considerable effort to locate the descendants of the author, I acquired the rights to republish a 1936 self-help book called *Wake Up and Live!* by Dorothea Brande. In this book, Brande writes that the pathology of human nature is what she called a *will to fail*. We fear failure and humiliation more than we crave success, so we constantly sabotage our plans in order to avoid the possibility of failure. We procrastinate. We make excuses. We blow important due dates or wreck professional relationships because we're more frightened of failure than we are hungry for success. But Brande further believed that if you were to *act as though it were impossible to fail*, you could bypass this self-negating pattern and achieve great things.

As mentioned, I spent a year trying to find her descendants so I could buy rights to this book, and

I finally did. After this effort, I learned of an audio publisher who wanted to issue out an audio edition. I do a lot of audio narration, although I was still just getting started at this point, and I told this publisher that I was eager to narrate this book. I had recorded for this publisher before. It had been successful and I thought, naturally they'll agree. But they wouldn't get back to me. My e-mails were ignored. My phone calls were ignored. I was very frustrated. I couldn't understand why they wouldn't want me to do this book. I was obviously brimming of passion for it. I had done good work before. But I just couldn't get anywhere. I was totally stuck. I was very frustrated. Finally the publisher replied to me with a decisive, "No."

I thought to myself, "Well, not only do I want to be doing more audiobooks, but this is the kind of book that I was born to read." I went into this exercise and I formed a mental picture. I'm not going to tell you what it was. It was too personal but it was also very simple. I formed a mental picture. I reviewed it faithfully two or three times a day for about two weeks.

Out of the clear blue, without any outer intervention on my part, a rights manager called to say, "Guess what? Someone else actually just bought the rights to that book. It's not with that audio publisher anymore. There's been a change. There's a new audio publisher." I said, "Please tell that new publisher that

I am dying to read this book." She got back to me. The new publisher said, "I sent Horowitz an e-mail a week ago asking him to read another audiobook and he never get back to me." I had gotten no such email. I went into my spam folder and found nothing. I went into a still deeper spam filter—and there is was. We signed a deal for me to narrate a total of three books, including *Wake Up and Live!*

I went from being ignored, to being told no, to signing a three-book narration deal. That relationship became one of the most central of my professional life. That same publisher issued this book that you are now reading. I did nothing to influence any of this in the outer world. I didn't do anything or contact anybody. I just did my visualization as Neville prescribed. It ended with the new audio publisher saying, "I contacted him a week ago. Why didn't he get back to me?"

For various reasons, this episode could be considered ordinary and I'm not oblivious to that. But I can say the following: from where I stood, and from long experience, it did not appear ordinary. "Take my challenge and put my words to the test. If the law does not work, its knowledge will not comfort you, and if it is not true, you must discard it. I hope you will be bold enough to test me" That's what Neville said over and over. You don't have to join anything. You don't have to buy anything. You can go online and listen to his lectures. Many of his books can be downloaded for free. His lectures can be downloaded for free. All he would insist is: "Put me to the test. Put me to the test."

Ecce Homo

Neville was born in 1905 on the island of Barbados, as mentioned. He was not born to a wealthy, landholding family. He was born to an Anglican family of merchants. He was one of ten children, nine boys and a girl. The family ran a food service and catering business, which later mushroomed into a highly profitable corporation. One of the things that I found about Neville is that the life details and events he claimed in his lectures often turned out to be verifiably true.

I've done a lot of work to track down and verify some of Neville's claims. He came to New York City to study theater and dancing in 1922. He didn't have any money. He was a poor kid and knocked about. He lived in a shared apartment on the Upper West Side on West 75th Street. His large family back home was not rich but over the course of time, they became very rich. They later put him on kind of an allowance or a monthly stipend. Much later, he was able to pursue his studies into the occult, into philosophy, into mysticism, completely independently.

Goddard Industries is today a major catering business in Barbados. They not only cater parties and events, but they cater for airlines. They cater for cruise ships and industrial facilities. By the standards of the West Indies, they're a large and thriving business. Everything that was said in his lectures about his family's growth in fortune is true. His father, Joe or Joseph, founded the business. Neville talks frequently about his older brother Victor, in his lectures. I'm not going to go into all the details here because I have a more exciting example that I want to bring to you, but everything that Neville described about the rise of his family's fortune matches business records and reportage in West Indian newspapers.

Neville lived in Greenwich Village for many years. In the 1940s he was at 32 Washington Square on the west side of Washington Square Park. He spent many years happily there. Now, here was a story that interested me in his lectures and I determined to track down the truth of it. Neville was drafted into the Army on November 12, 1942, just a little less than a year into America's entry to World War II, so it was at the height of war. Everybody was being drafted. He was a little old to be drafted. He was 37 at that time, but you could still be drafted up to age 45. He tells this story in several of his lectures.

He didn't want to be in the Army. He wanted no part of the war. He wanted to return home to Greenwich Village. At that time, he was married. He had a small daughter, Victoria or Vicky. He had a son from an earlier marriage. He wanted to go back to lecturing. He was in basic training in Louisiana. He asked his commanding officer for a discharge and the commanding officer definitively refused.

So Neville said that every night he would lay down in his cot and imagine himself back home in Greenwich Village, walking around Washington Square Park, back with his wife and family. Every night he'd go to bed in this sensation.

Night after night, he did this for several weeks. And he said that finally, out of the clear blue, the commanding officer came to him and said, "Do you still want to be discharged?" Neville said, "Yes, I do." "You're being honorably discharged," the officer told him.

As I read this, I doubted it. Why would the United States want to discharge a perfectly healthy, athletic male at the height of the America's entry into the Second World War? It made no sense. I started looking for Neville's military records to see if there were other things that would back this up. Neville claimed that he entered the military in late 1942 and then he was honorably discharged about four months later using nothing other than these mental-emotive techniques.

I found Neville's surviving military records. He was, in fact, inducted into the Army on November 12, 1942. I spoke to an Army public affairs spokesman who confirmed that Neville was honorably discharged in March 1943, which is the final record of his U.S. Army pay statement. The reason for the discharge in military records is that he had to return to a "vital civilian occupation." I said to the spokesman, "This man was a metaphysical lecturer, that is not seen as a vital civilian occupation." And he said to me, "Well, unfortunately, the rest of Mr. Goddard's records were destroyed in a fire at a military records facility 1973"—one year following Neville's death.

I know that Neville was back in New York City because *The New Yorker* magazine ran surprisingly extensive profile of him in September of 1943, which places him back on the circuit. He was depicted speaking all around town—in midtown in the Actor's Church, in Greenwich Village, and he completely resumed his career, this "vital civilian occupation" as a metaphysical lecturer. Now, I can't tell you what happened. I can only tell you that the forensics as he described them were accurate. This was one of several instances in which he describes an unlikely story, claims that he used his method as I've described it them you, and, while I can't tell you exactly what happened, I can tell you that the forensics line up.

Neville filled out an application for naturalization and citizenship on September 1, 1943. His address was 32 Washington Square at the time, his age 38 years old. Everything he described in terms of his whereabouts added up.

The Source

I want to say a quick word about where this philosophy came from. Where did Neville get these ideas? His thought was wholly original but everyone has antecedents of some kind. Neville was part of a movement that I call "the positive-thinking movement." Positive-mind metaphysics was a very American philosophy, and it was very much a homegrown philosophy, but, at the same time, every thought that's ever been thought has been encountered by sensitive people in the search extending back to the mythical Hermes, who ancient people in West and Near East considered the progenitor of all ideas and all intellect.

Hermetic philosophy was a Greek-Egyptian philosophy that was written about and set down in the Greek language in the city of Alexandria a few decades following the death of Christ. Neville quotes from one of the Hermetic books in the lecture "Inner Conversations" in this volume. A central Hermetic theme is that through proper preparation, diet, meditation, and prayer, the individual can be permeated by divine forces. This was a key tenet of Hermeticism. This outlook was reborn during the Renaissance when scholars and translators came to venerate the figure of Hermes Trismegistus, or thrice-greatest Hermes, a Greek term of veneration of Egypt's god of intellect Thoth. Hermes Trismegistus, a mythical man-god, was considered a great figure of antiquity by Renaissance thinkers, of a vintage as old as Moses or Abraham or older still.

Renaissance translators initially believed that the Hermetic literature—tracts that were signed by Hermes Trismegistus, whose name was adopted by Greek-Egyptian scribes—extended back to primeval antiquity. Hermetic writings were considered the source of earliest wisdom. This literature was later correctly dated to late antiquity. After the re-dating, Hermetic ideas eventually fell out of vogue. Some of the intellectual lights of the Renaissance had placed great hopes that the writings attributed to Hermes Trismegistus possessed great antiquity. And when those hopes of antiquity were and these writings were accurately dated to late antiquity, the readjustment of the timeline, I think tragically for Western civilization, convinced many people that the whole project of the Hermetic literature was somehow compromised. For that reason there are, to this day, relatively few quality translations of the Hermetic literature. The dating issue assumed too great a proportion in people's minds. The fact is, all ancient literature, just like all religions, are built from earlier ideas, and I believe the Hermetic philosophy was a retention of much older oral philosophy. Most scholars today agree with that.

In any case, the Hermetic ideas faded. Including the core principle that the human form could be permeated by something higher and could itself attain a kind of creative and clairvoyant power. These ideas that were so arousing, that created such hope and intrigue during Renaissance, got pushed to the margins. But they eventually reentered the public mind in part through the influence of Franz Anton Mesmer (1734-1815), who was a lawyer and a self-styled physician of Viennese descent. Mesmer appeared in Paris in 1778, in the decade preceding the French Revolution. He entered into royal courts with this radical theory that all of life was animated by this invisible etheric fluid which he called *animal magnetism*.

Mesmer maintained that if you place an individual into a kind of trance state, what we would call a hypnotic trance—recall Neville talking about this state of drowsiness, this hypnagogic state—you could then realign his or her animal magnetism, this ethereal life fluid, and cure physical or mental diseases, and, according to practitioners, introduce powers such as clairvoyance or the ability to speak in unknown foreign tongues. You could heal. You could empower. You could get at the life stuff of the individual. I was recently in a Walgreen's drugstore and saw an ad reading, "Mysterious and Mesmerizing," for a skin lotion. It's funny how occult language, unmoored from its meaning, lingers in daily life.

Mesmer was feted in royal courts but his philosophy aroused suspicion. At the instigation of King Louis XVI, Mesmerism was discredited by a royal commission in 1784. This investigatory commission was chaired by Benjamin Franklin, who at the time was America's ambassador to France. The commission concluded that there was no such thing as animal magnetism and that whatever cures or effects were experienced under the influence of a mesmeric trance were "in the imagination." But there the committee left dangling its most extraordinary question. If it's "in the imagination," why should there be any effects at all?

Mesmer's greatest students edged away from the idea of animal magnetism as some physical, ethereal fluid. They believed something else was at work. In their struggle for answers, they arrived at the first descriptions of what we would later call subliminal mind and then the subconscious or unconscious mind. Mesmer's proteges did not possess a psychological vocabulary—they preceded and in some regards prefigured modern psychology—but they knew that *something* was evident and effective in his theory of animal magnetism. The best students morphed the master's theories into an early, rough iteration of the subconscious mind. This is an overlooked and crucial basis for the growth of modern psychology. The terms subliminal and subconscious mind began to be heard in the 1890s.

Mesmer died in 1815. But his ideas were taken up in many quarters including, fatefully, by a New England clockmaker named Phineas Quimby (1802-1866). Starting in the late 1830s, Quimby began to experiment with how states of *personal excitement* could make him feel better physically. Quimby suffered from tuberculosis and he discovered that when he would take vigorous carriage rides in the Maine countryside, the effects of tuberculosis would lift. Quimby began to probe the state of his mood and the state of his physical wellbeing. He treated others and became known as a mental healer in the mid-1840s.

At first, Quimby worked with a teenaged boy named Lucius Burkmar. Lucius would enter a trance or hypnagogic state from which he was said to be able to clairvoyantly view people's bodily organs and diagnose and prescribe cures for diseases.

Quimby discovered that sometimes the cures that Lucius prescribed, which were often botanical remedies or herbal teas, had previously been prescribed by physicians—and did not work. But when Lucius prescribed them, *they often did work*. The difference, Quimby concluded, was in the *confidence of the patient*. Quimby stopped working with Lucius and encouraged patients to arouse mental energies on their own.

American medicine in the mid-1840s was in a horrendously underdeveloped state. It was the one area of the sciences in which American lagged behind Europe. People had some reason to be driven to mental healers and prayer healers because, if anything, they were less dangerous than most of what was then standard allopathic medicine, which involved measures that were medieval. Physicians were performing bloodletting, administering mercury and other poisons and narcotics. At the very least, the mental healing movement caused no harm.

And, according to historical letters, articles, and diaries, sometimes it did a lot of good. Someone who briefly served as a student to Quimby was Mary Baker Eddy (1821–1921), who founded her own movement called Christian Science. Eddy taught that the healing ministry of Christ is an ever-present fact that is still going on on Earth, and that individuals could be healed by the realization that there is only one true reality and that is this great divine mind that created the universe and that animates everything around us; and further that matter, these forms that we live in, and the floorboards underneath our feet, are not real. They are illusory, as are illness, prejudice, violence, and all human corruption. Eddy taught that through prayer and proper understanding of Scripture, the individual could be healed. She was a remarkable figure. Sometimes people will say, in a far too hasty way, "Well, she took all her ideas from Quimby." It's not that simple. Her interlude with Quimby in the early 1860s was vitally important in her development; but her ideas were uniquely her own. She was an extraordinary figure. I don't think we've taken full measure in this culture of how influential Mary Baker Eddy's ideas have been.

Another figure who become indirectly influential in this healing movement was Emanuel Swedenborg (1688–1772), a Swedish scientist and mystic who worked primarily in the 1700s. Swedenborg's central idea was that the mind is a conduit, a capillary, of cosmic laws, and everything that occurs in the world, including our own thoughts, mirrors events in an invisible world, a spiritual world, which we do not see but always interact with. Everything that men and women do on Earth, Swedenborg taught, is a reflection of something occurring in this unseen world, and our minds are almost like receiving stations, spiritual telegraphs, for messages and ideas from a cosmic plane in which we cannot directly participate but are vitally linked.

Swedenborg was an influence on a Methodist minister named Warren Felt Evans, who was also a contemporary of Quimby's, and who briefly worked with him. Evans wrote a book in 1869 called *The Mental Cure* which was the first book to use the term "new age" in the spiritual sense that it's used today. Evans believed that through prayer, proper direction of thought, use of affirmations, and assumption of a confident mental state, the individual could be cured. *The Mental Cure* is not read anywhere today. Yet it is a surprisingly sprightly book. You'd be surprised. When I first had to read *The Mental Cure* I braced myself but I found that its pages turn quite effortlessly. Evans was a brilliant writer. All of his books are obscure today. But he was a seminal figure in the creation of a positive-thinking movement.

More indirectly, the British poet William Blake also had a certain influence on this movement, and on Neville in particular. Blake believed that humans dwell in this coarse world where we are imprisoned in a fortress of illusions; but the one true mind, the great creative imagination of God, can course through us. We can "cleanse the doors of perception." We can feel the coursing of this great mind within us.

These are some of the same ideas that resounded in Hermeticism. There wasn't a direct connection, necessarily. First of all, there weren't many translations of some of the Hermetic literature, which a man like Blake could likely draw upon. People from different epochs and eras often arrived at these parallel cosmic ideas themselves. When academic writers approach New Thought or the positive-thinking movement, they sometimes make the mistake of conflating it with the idealist philosophy of figures like Berkeley, Kant, Hegel, and later Schopenhauer and Nietzsche. The positive-thinking figures were not directly influenced by the idealists. Those figures and their phraseology are absent in early positive-mind writings. People sometimes make the mistake of not realizing that in a country like America, which was a very agricultural country throughout most of the 19th century, little of this material was directly available.

As an example, consider the Tao Te Ching. This great ancient Chinese work on ethics and philosophy wasn't even translated into English until 1838. In the mid-1840s, there existed four English-language copies in all of the United States. One was in the library at Harvard, one was in Ralph Waldo Emerson's library which he lent out, and two were in private hands. It wasn't like somebody like Phineas Quimby, the New England clockmaker, who was experimenting with moods and the body, could locate Taoist or Hermetic philosophy, or could even read translations of Hegel. Literacy aside, many of these things weren't accessible. It's a mistake to conclude that because one system of thought mirrors another, that the preceding system is necessarily the birth mother of the later one. In the rural environs of America, many of the positive-mind theorists were independently coming up with these ideas.

Moving into the 20th century, we encounter a figure who directly influenced Neville—French mind theorist Emile Coué (1857-1926). Coué was a largely self-trained hypnotherapist. He died in 1926, but shortly before he died, he made two lecture tours of the United States. Coué was hugely popular in the US and in England. He had a key theory, which rested on the principle that when you enter a sleepy drowsy state, the hypnagogic state, your mind is uniquely supple, suggestible, and powerful. Coué came up with a method to use in conjunction with this state. His system was so simple that critics mocked it. You've probably heard of it. Coué told people to gently repeat the mantra, "Day by day, in every way, I am getting better and better." He said you should lay in bed and recite this just as you're drifting off at night and again just as you're coming to in the morning. Whisper it twenty times to your-self. You could knot a piece of string twenty times and take that piece of string with you, keep it at your bedside, so you could count off your repetitions like a rosary.

Coué had many thousands of followers, but he also became a figure of ridicule because the crit-ics said: "How could such a simple idea possibly do anything for anyone?" Of course, they would not try it. To their minds, it was *prima facie* nonsense. Such an attitude reminds me of the character of Dr. Zaius from *Planet of the Apes* insisting that flight is a physical impossibility. Thought in the absence of experience is the impoverishment of our intellec-tual culture. Certainty in the absence of personal experience precludes effort.

In addition to the uses of hypnagogia, another of Coué's ideas appeared in Neville's thought system. You can find the language from time to time in Nev-ille's lectures and writing. (I've given two examples in the introduction.) That is, within human beings exist two forces: *will* and *imagination*. The *will* is intel-lectual self-determination. The *imagination* is the mental images and emotionally conditioned reactions that populate our psyches, particularly with regard to self-image. Coué said that when imagination and will are in conflict, *imagination always win*. Your emotional state always overcomes your intellect.

As an example, Coué said, place a wooden plank on the floor and ask an average person to walk across it. He or she will have no problem. But if you raise that same wooden plank twenty feet off the ground, in many cases the person will be petrified even though there's no difference in the physical demand. They are capable of walking across it. The risk of falling is minimal. *The change in condition alone creates an emotional state that makes them more nervous and hence accident prone.* Coué believed it necessary to cultivate new imaginative images of ourselves. We cannot do that through the intellect alone. But we can do so by making using of this very subtle hypnagogic state. He called his method auto-suggestion. It was self-hypnosis essentially. Neville adopted the method, if not the same assumptions behind it.

The Mystic in Life

There are few pictures of Neville. His smiles glowingly in rare pictures toward the end of his life. He died young at age 67 in 1972. He died of heart failure in West Hollywood where he was living with his family. Until the end, his voice and his powers of communication never left him. They absolutely resonated.

It's interesting sometimes to look at the lives of mystical figures like Neville who are hard to pin down, but who did lead domestic lives. There was a little piece in the *Los Angeles Times* on October 21, 1962: "Ms. Goddard Named as College President." It went on, "Miss Victoria Goddard, daughter of Mr. and Mrs. Neville Goddard, has been appointed co-chairman of campus publicity by the student government president at Russell Sage College for New York. She is an English major." This was Neville's daughter.

Now, Victoria Goddard or Vicky as she's known, is still living. She lives in Los Angeles in the family house that she once resided in with her parents. She avoids publicity and contact with people who are interested in Neville's ideas. I've tried to reach out to her but she has no interest in being in touch. She did give her approval indirectly to an anthology of Neville's writings that I wrote an introduction to, but she doesn't want contact with his students. She wants to lead her own existence. But it's funny sometimes we come across little things like this article or a photograph and realize that every one of us share the same workaday concerns.

For all of Neville's wonderful mystical theories, I just have to share this little discourse that he went into about Liquid-Plumr in a lecture that he delivered in 1970. I found this a delightful reminder of how the ordinary steps into all of our lives even when we're trying to deal with cosmic and mystical concerns. He told an audience in 1970:

So you buy something because of highly publicized TV promotions. Someone highly publicized what is called "Liquid-Plumr." And so I had some moment in my bathroom where the sink was all stopped up, so I got the Liquid-Plumr. Poured it in, in abundance. It said it's heavier than water, and it would go all the way down and just eat up everything that is organic and will not hurt anything that is not organic, so I poured it in. Water still remained; it didn't go down. Called the plumber the next day. He couldn't come that day but he would come the next day. So it was forty-eight hours. So when he came the entire sink was eaten away by the Liquid-Plumr. So I asked him: "Does this thing work?" He said: "It does for two people: the one who manufactures it, and the one who sells it." They are the only ones who profit by the Liquid-Plumr. And so you turned on the TV and you saw it and you bought it. It is still on TV and I am sinning, because to sin by silence when I should protest makes cowards of us all. But I haven't protested to the station that advertises this nonsense and I haven't protested to the place where I got it or to anyone who manufactures it, so I am the silent sinner. Multiply me because of my embarrassment. Here is a sink completely eaten up by Liquid-Plumer.

"The silent sinner," he called himself. I lodge letters of protest and phone calls from time to time, so I can sympathize with everything Neville says here.

Neville published a variety of books during his lifetime, most of them quite short. There was a company in Los Angeles called G and J Publishing which issued most of his books. A symbol appeared on most of his covers, which he devised himself. It was a heart with an eye to symbolize eternal vision, inner vision, and it was part of a fruit-bearing tree. As the emotive state of man conceives, so the tree brings forth fruit.

In 1964, Neville published an extremely rare pamphlet called, *He Breaks The Shell*. On its cover you can see a little cherub or angelic figure coming out of a human head. Neville described this mystical experience and said that this is an experience that all of us will have either in this lifetime or another; and that the whole purpose of human existence is to be reborn from your imagination; and your imagination, as we experience it, is physically lodged in your skull, entombed in this kind of a womb. Christ was crucified in Golgotha, place of the skull. Neville believed that we each will be reborn from within our own skull, and that we will have an actual physical experience, maybe in the form of a dream, but a vivid, tactile experience of being reborn from out of the base of our skull. We will know, in that moment, that we are fulfilling our essential purpose.

He described this quite vividly. He had this experience in New York City in 1959 where he had an enormously tactile, sensationally real dream of being reborn from out of the skull. Minerva was said to have been reborn from the skull of Zeus or Jupiter. Christ was crucified at the place of the skull. "You and I," Neville said, "will be reborn from within our skull." In the late 1960s a booking agent told him, "Listen, you've got to stop telling this story at your talks. It's freaking everyone out. People want to hear the get-rich stuff." He told Neville that he if did not change course he'd have no audience left. "Then I'll tell it to the bare walls," Neville replied. He spoke of his mystical experience for the rest of his career until he died in 1972.

I reissued one of Neville's books recently, *The Power of Awareness*. I felt that, for the first time, Neville's books needed to be packaged in a way that fits their dignity, and this is a beautiful edition that I took great joy in working on because I thought it represented him with the right degree of dignity.

I want to quote from Neville's voice. He spoke in such beautiful, resonant language, so unhaltingly, never a pause, never an uncertainty. He knew his outlook so well, he could share it effortlessly. Here is his voice.

So I'm telling you of the power within you and that power is your own wonderful human imagination. And that is the only God in the world. There is no other God. That is the Jesus Christ of Scripture, so tonight take it seriously. If you really have an objective in this world and you're waiting for something to happen on the outside to make it so, forget it. Do it in your own wonderful human imagination. Actually bring it into being in your own imagination. Conjure a scene which would imply the fulfillment of that dream and lose yourself in the action as you contemplate it, and completely lose yourself in that state. If you're completely absorbed in it, you will objectify it and you will see it seemingly independent of your perception of it. But even if you do not have that intensity, if you lose yourself in it and feel it to true—the imaginal act—then drop it. In a way you do not know, it will become true.

If you are interested in hearing more of Neville, you can go online and find lectures that are posted on YouTube and almost everywhere. He allowed people who came to presentations to tape record them and freely distribute them. He claimed copyright over nothing, and that, to me, is the mark of a real leader. That's the mark of a real thinker. You don't have to join anything. You don't have to ask anybody permission for anything. You don't have to pay any dues. You don't have to buy anything. You just start.

Neville's Circle

I want to say a quick word about some of the people who have been influenced by Neville today. One of them is the major-league baseball pitcher, Barry Zito, who actually introduced me to Neville. I was doing an article about Barry in 2003 and he said to me, "Oh, you must be into Neville," and I said, "I've never heard of him." He said, "Really? You never heard of him?" He was the first one who got me interested in Neville's thought, and that was a huge influence in my life. It was almost 10 years ago to this very day and in many regards put me where I am today.

The New Age writer Wayne Dyer wrote a lot about Neville in his most recent book which is called *Wishes Fulfilled*. But a really remarkable influence that Neville brought into the world came in the form his subtle impact on the writer, Carlos Castaneda, of whom I'm a great admirer. I want to read a short passage from my forthcoming book, *One Simple Idea*:

By the mid-1950s, Neville's life story exerted a powerful pull on a budding writer whose own memoirs of mystic discovery later made him a near-household name: Carlos Castaneda. Castaneda told his own tales of tutelage under a mysterious instructor, in his case a Native American sorcerer named Don Juan. Castaneda first discovered Neville through an early love interest in Los Angeles, Margaret Runyan, who was among Neville's most dedicated students. A cousin of American storyteller Damon Runyon, Margaret wooed the stocky Latin art student at a friend's house, slipping Carlos a slender Neville volume called *The Search,* in which she had inscribed her name and phone number. The two became lovers and later husband and wife. Runyan spoke frequently to Castaneda about her mystical teacher Neville, but he responded with little more than mild interest—with one exception.

In her memoirs, Runyan recalled Castaneda growing fascinated when the conversation turned to Neville's discipleship under an exotic teacher. She wrote:

> It was more than the message that attracted Carlos, it was Neville himself. He was so mysterious. Nobody was really sure who he was or where he had come from. There were vague references to Barbados in the West Indies and his being the son of an ultra-rich plantation family, but nobody knew for sure. They couldn't even be sure about

this Abdullah business, his Indian teacher, who was always way back there in the jungle, or someplace. The only thing you really knew was that Neville was here and that he might be back next week, but then again . . .

"There was," Runyon concluded, "a certain power in that position, an appealing kind of freedom in the lack of past and Carlos knew it."

Carlos knew it. Both Neville and Castaneda were dealing the same basic idea, and one that has a certain pedigree in America's alternative spiritual culture: tutelage under hidden spiritual masters.

Neville again and again told this story, that there was a turbaned black man of Jewish descent who tutored him starting in 1931 in kabbalah, Scripture, number symbolism, and mental metaphysics. He described Abdullah as this somewhat taciturn, mysterious figure who he met one day at a metaphysical lecture in 1931. Neville walked in and Abdullah said to him, "Neville, you're six months late." Neville said, "I had never seen this man before." Abdullah continued, "The brothers told me you were coming and you're six months late." He said they spent the next five years together studying.

Neville had his first true awakening experience in the winter of 1933. He was dying to get out of the Manhattan winter. He wanted to spend Christmas back home with his family in Barbados. He had no money and Abdullah said to him, "Walk the streets of Manhattan as if you are there and you shall be." And so Neville said he would walk the gray wintry streets of the Upper West Side with the feeling that he was in the palm-lined lanes of Barbados. He would go to see Abdullah, telling him, "It isn't working. I'm still here." And Abdullah would slam the door in his face and say, "You're not here. You're in Barbados."

Then one day, before the last ship departed for Barbados, his brother, Victor, from out of the blue, without any physical intercession on Neville's part, sent him a first-class steamer ticket and $50. "Come spend winter with us in Barbados," he wrote. Neville said he was transformed by the experience. He felt that it was Abdullah's law of mental assumption came to his rescue.

Now, this idea of mysterious spiritual masters got popularized in modern Western culture through the influence of Madame Blavatsky and her partner Colonel Henry Steel Olcott who founded the movement of Theosophy in New York City in 1975. They claimed to be under the tutelage of hidden spiritual masters, Master Koot Hoomi, who was said to be Tibetan, and Master Morya who was said to be Indian. These adepts, they said, would send them phenomenally produced letters, advising them what to do, giving them directions, giving them advice, giving them succor. Around that time, Colonel Olcott and Madame Blavatsky were living in a building which is still standing at the corner of 8th Avenue of West 47th Street which was known as the Lamasery, their headquarters or salon, where they dwelt on the second floor. Today it is an Econo Lodge. None of the people who worked there were very entranced with my attempts to explain the history of the building.

Colonel Olcott said that one time in the winter of 1877, Master Morya materialized in his room and directed him and Madame Blavatsky to relocate to the nation of India, which they did the following year. They helped instigate the Indian independence movement. Olcott went on speaking tours all over the Near East, Far East, Japan, Sri Lanka. He helped instigate a rebirth of Buddhism throughout the East. Blavatsky and Olcott were enormously effective in their way. Colonel Olcott attributed all of it to the presence of these mysterious spiritual masters, these great turbaned figures somewhere from the East who had given them instruction.

Now, I first wrote about Neville in an article that was published in February 2005 in *Science of Mind* magazine called "Searching for Neville Goddard." Things had been fairly quiet around Neville for many years, and that article attracted a lot of interest. I started receiving phone calls and e-mail after e-mail asking me, who was Abdullah? Did he exist? Could he be identified? I would tell people at the time that I thought Abdullah was a kind of a mythos that Neville might have borrowed, clipped and pasted, from Theosophy. I didn't think there was any evidence to show that Abdullah was a real person, and I thought the dramatic claims around him were probably Neville's mythmaking.

Now, to my surprise, I discovered something about Abdullah through another figure in the positive thinking movement, a man named Joseph Murphy, who died in 1981, and who wrote a very popular book, which some of you may have read, called *The Power of Your Subconscious Mind*. Shortly before his death, Murphy gave a series of interviews to a French-speaking minister from Quebec. The interviewer published his book only in French with Quebec press. It is called *Dialogues with Joseph Murphy* and in these interviews Murphy offhandedly remarks that he, too, was a student of Abdullah. Murphy actually came to New York around the same time as Neville in 1922. He migrated from Ireland. Murphy worked as a pharmacist at the Algonquin Hotel. They used to have a little pharmacy in their lobby. And Murphy also became a metaphysical lecturer and was acquainted with Neville for several years. He stated very simply and matter-of-factly that Abdullah was his teacher too, and that he was a very real man.

I began to look around and correspond with people, and I came to feel, over the past few years, that I happened upon a figure who might actually be Abdullah. He was Arnold Josiah Ford. Ford was a mystic, black nationalist, and part of a movement called the Black Hebrew Movement which still exists in various forms. Ford was born in Barbados, Neville's home island, in 1877. Ford emigrated to Harlem in 1910. He became involved with Marcus Garvey's Universal Negro Improvement Association, of which he was musical director. In surviving photographs Ford, like Abdullah, is turbaned.

In addition to being a dedicated follower of Marcus Garvey—who had his own mind-power metaphysics, about which I'll say a quick word in a moment—Ford was also part of a movement called Ethiopianism. It was a precursor to Rastafarianism. Ford believed, as the Rastafarian people do, as many other people do with good reason, that Ethiopia, one of the oldest continuous civilizations on Earth and one of the most populous nations in Africa, was home to a lost tribe of Israel, which, in this line of teaching, had its own blend of what we know as traditional historical Judaism and mystical teachings and mental metaphysics.

The movement of Ethiopianism believed that this lost African-Israelite tribe harbored a great wealth of ancient teachings that had been lost to most modern people. The Ethiopianism movement believed in mind-power metaphysics and mental healing. Ford was considered a rabbi and he had his own African-American congregation in Harlem. He described himself a man of authentic Israelite and Jewish descent. Writing in 1946, occult philosopher Israel Regardie described Neville's Abdullah as an "Ethiopian rabbi." Regardie, who had been a secretary to the occultist, Aleister Crowley, is quoted on Neville in the introduction.

According to census records, Ford was living in Harlem 1931. He identified his occupation to the census taker as rabbi. That was the same year that Neville met Abdullah. (Although he later gave Abdullah's address as the Upper West Side, not Harlem.) Neville may have been playing around with the name a little bit. He would affectionately refer to Abdullah in his lectures as *Ab*. Ab is a variant of the Hebrew word *abba* for father. Perhaps he saw Abdullah, Ford, as kind of a father figure. He said they studied metaphysics, Scripture, Kabbalah together for five years. Ford has been written about in histories of the Black Hebrew Movement as a key figure who brought authentic knowledge of the Hebrew language, Talmud, and Kabbalah into the Black Hebrew Movement as it existed in Harlem at that time.

Ford was a person of some learning. He was, as I said, a follower of Marcus Garvey, a figure about whom I write in *Occult America*. Garvey has not been properly understood in our culture. He was a pioneering black nationalist figure. He was a great pioneering activist and voice of liberation. He was also very much into his own brand of mental metaphysics. You might recognize this statement of Garvey's which Bob Marley adapted in the lyrics to *Redemption Song:* "We are going to emancipate ourselves from mental slavery because whilst others might free the body, none but ourselves can free the mind." Garvey's speeches are shot through with New Thought language, with the language of mental metaphysics. This was an essential part of Garvey's outlook. This perspective was also essential to the culture of Ethiopianism, which saw Ethiopia's crowned emperor, Haile Selassie, who was coronated in 1930, as a messianic figure. The movement of Ethiopianism morphed into Rastafarianism. It started in the mid-1930s.

Now, there are a lot of correspondences between Arnold Josiah Ford and Neville's description of Abdullah, including physical correspondences, the turban and such. But for all that I've noted, the timeline does not match up sufficiently to make any of this conclusive; because Ford left America sometime in 1931, and he moved to the Ethiopian countryside. After Haile Selassie was coronated as emperor, he offered a land grant to any African-American willing to emigrate to Ethiopia. The emperor saw Ethiopia in a way that matched Ford's ideals as a kind of African-Israel. Haile Selassie wanted Afro-Caribbean and Afro-American people to move, or to come home as he saw it, to Ethiopia, so he offered land grants.

Ford and about thirty followers of Ethiopianism in New York accepted the land grants. There's been some debate about when Ford left, but I have a *New York Times* article that places Ford in New York City still in December 1930. He didn't leave until 1931. That was the same year that Neville said they met. The timeline doesn't match up because Neville said they studied together for five years, so it's possible that Ford was one of several teachers that Neville had, and he created a kind of composite figure who he called Abdullah, Ab, father, of whom Ford may have been a part.

Now, in a coda to Ford's life, I must take note that it was a tougher and braver and more brutal existence back then in some regards. Ford, who for 20 years has been living as a musician and a rabbi in Harlem, moved to rural Ethiopia, the northern part of this nation, to accept Haile Selassie's land grant. He died there in 1935. Tragically, there are no records of Ford's life in Ethiopia. It must have been very difficult. Imagine being a metropolitan person and uprooting yourself to a completely rural setting in a developing nation in the 1930s, and Mussolini is beating the war drum, and Mussolini's fascist troops invaded Ethiopia just weeks after Ford's death, across the north border. This was a man who put himself through tremendous ordeals for his principles. I cannot conclude that Ford was Abdullah. But Murphy's testimony suggests that there *was* an Abdullah, and I think Ford corresponds in many ways—and I write about this in *One Simple Idea*; there probably is some intersection there.

There's another figure I want to mention of a very different kind whose thought had some indirect intersection with Neville's, and that is Aleister Crowley, the British occultist. Crowley made a very interesting statement in a book that he received in a way that we might call channeled perception in 1904; it was later published broadly in 1938 called *The Book of the Law*. In this introduction, Crowley writes:

> Each of us has thus an universe of his own, but it is the same universe for each one as soon as it includes all possible experience. This implies the extension of consciousness to include all other consciousnesses. In our present stage, the object that you see is never the same as the one that I see; we infer that it is the same because your experience tallies with mine on so many points

that the actual differences of our observation are negligible . . . Yet all the time neither of us can know anything . . . at all beyond the total impression made on our respective minds.

Neville said something similar:

Do you realize that no two people live in the same world? We may be together now in this room, but we will go home tonight and close our doors on entirely different worlds. Tomorrow, we will go to work where we'll meet others but each one of us lives in our own mental and physical world.

Neville meant this in the most literal sense. He believed that every individual, possessed of his or her own imagination, is God, and that everyone you see, including me standing in this room, is rooted in you, as you are ultimately rooted in God.

You exist in this world of infinite possibilities and realities, and that, in fact, when you mentally picture something, you're not creating it—it already exists. You're claiming it. The very fact of being able to experience it mentally confirms that in this world of infinite possibilities, where imagination is the ultimate creative agent, everything that you can picture *already is*.

Mind Science

Some of the things that Neville said prefigured studies both in psychical research and quantum physics. I want to say a quick word about that. One of
my heroes is, J.B. Rhine, a psychical researcher who
performed tens of thousands of trials at Duke Uni-
versity in the 1930s and beyond to test for clairvoyant perception. Rhine often used a five-suit deck of
cards called Zener cards; if you were guessing a card,
you had a one-in-five chance, 20 percent, of nam-
ing the right card. As Rhine documented in literally
tens of thousands of trials, with meticulous clinical
control, certain individuals persistently, under controlled conditions, scored higher than a chance hit
of 20 percent.

It wasn't always dramatically higher. It wasn't
like Zeus was aiming lightning bolts at the Earth.
But if someone over the course of thousands of trials keeps scoring 25 percent, 26 percent, 27 percent,
beyond all chance possibility, and the results are
parsed, juried, gone over, reviewed, you have some
anomalous transfer of information going on in a labo-
ratory setting. Rhine's research was real. And Rhine
noticed—and he had this quietly monumental way
of describing things, he would make some observation in a footnote that could be extraordinary—that

the correlation to a high success rate of hits on the Zener cards was usually a feeling of enthusiasm, positive expectation, hopefulness, belief in the possibility of ESP, and an encouraging environment. Then when boredom or physical exhaustion would set in, or interest would wane, the results would go down. If interest was somehow renewed, revised, if there was a feeling of comity in the testing room, the results would go up.

We as a culture haven't begun to deal with the implications of Rhine's experiments. There was another parapsychologist, Charles Honorton, who began a series of experiments in 1970s—I see him as Rhine's successor—called the *ganzfeld* experiments. Ganzfeld is German for whole field. Honorton experimented on subjects who were in a hypnagogic state, the state of drowsiness. Honorton and his collaborators theorized that if you could induce the near-sleep state in an individual, put somebody in conditions of comfortable isolation, fit them with eye coverings and headphones emitting white noise or some kind of negative sound to listen to, put them in a greatly relaxed state, it might be possible to heighten the appearance of some kind of clairvoyant faculty.

His test was to place a subject, a receiver, into a comfortable isolation tank, and to place another subject, a sender, in a different room. Then the sender attempted to mentally convey an image—

such as a flower, a rocket, a boat, or something else—to the receiver, and see what happens. These tests generally used four images. Three were decoys, one was actual. Again, in certain subjects, and also in the subjects as a whole in the form of meta-analysis, Honorton found over and over again results that showed a higher than 25 percent chance hit when subjects were placed into the hypnagogic state.

We're in this state all the time. When you're napping, when you're dozing off at your desk, when you're going to sleep at night, when you're waking up in the morning. Neville's message is: *use it.* Honorton died very young in 1992 at age 46. He had suffered health problems his whole life. If he had lived, his name would, I believe, be as well-known as J.B. Rhine. He was a great parapsychologist.

There's another field burgeoning today called neuroplasticity that relates to some of Neville's sights. In short, brain imaging shows that repeat thoughts change the pathways through which electrical impulses travel in your brain. This has been used to treat obsessive compulsive disorder. A research psychologist named Jeffery Schwartz at UCLA has devised a program that ameliorates and dissipates obsessive thoughts. Schwartz's program teaches patients and people in his clinical trials to substitute something in place of an obsessive thought at the very moment they experience it. This diversion may be a pleasurable physical activity, listening to music, jogging, whatever they want, just anything that gets them off that obsessive thought. Schwartz has found through brain imaging, and many scientists have replicated this data, that if you repeat an exercise like that, eventually biologic changes manifest in the brain, neuropathways change, thoughts themselves alter brain biology as far as electrical impulses are concerned.

A New Thought writer in 1911, who theorized without any of the contemporary brain imaging and neuroscience, came up with exactly the same prescription. His name was John Henry Randall. Randall called it *substitution*. His language and the language used today by 21st century researchers in neuroplasticity is extraordinarily similar.

Finally, we have emerging from the field of quantum physics an extraordinary set of questions, which have been coming at us actually for 80-plus years, about the extent to which observation influences the manifestation of subatomic particles. I want to give a very brief example. Basically, quantum physics experiments have shown that if you direct a wave of particles, often in the form of a light wave, at a target system, perhaps a double-slit box or two boxes, the wave of light will collapse into a particle state, it will go from a wave state to a particle state. This occurs when a conscious observer is present or a measurement is occurring. Interference patterns demonstrate that the particle-like properties of wave of light *at one time appeared in both boxes*. Only when someone decided to look or to take a measurement did the particles become localized in one box.

In 1935, physicist Erwin Schrodinger noted that the conclusions of these quantum experiments were so outrageous, were so contrary to all observed experience, that he devised a thought experiment called Schrodinger's Cat in order to highlight this surreality. Schrodinger did not intend his thought experiment to endorse quantum theorizing. He intended it to compel quantum theorists to deal with the ultimate and, what he considered, absurdist conclusions of their theories—theories which have never been overturned, theories which have been affirmed for 80 years. Now, Schrodinger's Cat comes down to this, it can be put this way: You take two boxes. You put a cat into one of the two boxes. You direct a subatomic particle at the boxes. One box is empty, one box holds the cat. Inside the box with the cat is what he called a "diabolical device." This diabolical device trips a beaker of poison when it comes in contact with a subatomic particle, thus killing the cat.

So, you do your experiment. You direct the particle and you go to check the boxes. Which box is the particle in? Is the cat dead? Is the cat alive? The cat is *both*, Schrodinger insisted. It must be *both* because the subatomic particle can be shown to exist in more than one place, in a wave state, until someone checks, and thus localizes it into a particle state, occupying one place. Hence, you must allow for both outcomes— you have a dead/alive cat. That makes no sense. All of lived experience says that you've got two boxes; you've got one cat; the cat's dead if you fired into the box with the cat; or the cat's alive if you fired into the other box. Schrodinger said, "Not so." Interference experiments demonstrate that at one point the sub-atomic particle was in a *wave state*; it was non-local; it existed only in potential; it existed in both boxes and, given the nature of quantum observation, potentially everywhere. It is only when you go to check and open one of the boxes that the particle becomes localized. *It was in both boxes until a conscious observer made the decision to check.*

A later group of physicists argued there's no doubting Schrodinger's conclusion, and in fact, if you were to check eight hours later, you would not only find a cat that was living/dead, but you would find a living cat that was hungry because it hadn't been fed for eight hours. The timing itself created a past, present, and future for the cat—a reality selected out of infinite possibilities. Schrodinger didn't intend for his thought experiment to affirm this radical departure from reality. He intended it to expose what he considered the absurdist conclusions of quantum physics. But quantum physics data kept mounting and mounting, and Schrodinger's thought experiment became to some physicists a very real illustration of the extraordinary physical impossibilities that we were seeing in the world of quantum physics.

The implication is that we live in a serial universe—that there are infinite realities, whether we experience them or not; and our experience of one of these realties rests on observation. If we can extrapolate from the extraordinary behaviors of subatomic particles, it stands to reason that parallel events and potentials are all are occurring simultaneously. Why don't we experience any of this? Our world is seemingly controlled by Newtonian mechanics. There aren't dead/alive cats. There are singular events. Why don't we experience quantum reality?

Today, a theory that makes the rounds among quantum physicists that when something gets bigger and bigger—remember these experiments are done on subatomic particles, the smallest isolated fragments of matter—when we pull back from a microscopic view of things, we experience what is known as "information leakage." The world gets less and less clear as it gets bigger; as we exit the subatomic level and enter the mechanical level that is familiar, we lose information about what's really going on.

American philosopher William James made the same observation in 1902. James said that when you view an object under a microscope, you're getting so much information; but more and more of that information is lost as you pan back. This is true of all human experience. A cohort of quantum physicists today says the same thing: that the actions of the particle lab are occurring around us always, but we don't know it because we lose information in this coarse physical world that we live in.

Neville said something similar. He said that you radiate the world around you by the persuasiveness of your imagination and feelings. A quantum physicist might call this observation. But in our three-dimensional world, Neville said, time beats so slowly that we do not always observe the relationship between the visible world and our inner nature. You and I can contemplate a desire and become it, but because of the slowness of time, it is easy to forget what we formerly set out to worship or destroy. Quantum physicists speak of "information leakage;" Neville basically spoke of "time leakage." Time moves so slowly for us that we lose the sense of cause and effect.

"Scientists will one day explain why there is a serial universe," Neville said in 1948, "but in practice, how you use the serial universe to change the future is more important."

TRY

I want to leave you with a slogan of an American occultist P.B. Randolph who lived in New York City. He was a man of African-American descent and a tremendously original thinker and mystical experimenter. He died at the young age of 49 in 1875. This was his personal slogan: *TRY.* That's all. *TRY.* This slogan later appeared in letters signed by the spiritual masters Koot Hoomi and Morya, which started reaching Colonel Henry Steel Olcott in 1870s. The first appeared about two months before Randolph's death. The letters used the same slogan: *TRY.*

What you're hearing now is something to try. Neville's challenge was as ultimate as it was simple: "Put my ideas to the test." Prove them to yourself or dismiss them, but what a tragedy would be not to try. It's all so simple.

I want to conclude with words from William Blake, who was one of Neville's key inspirations later in life. Blake described the coarsened world of the senses that we live in. He described such things sometimes in matters of geography. When he would say England, he didn't mean England the nation exactly. He meant the coarse world in which men and women find themselves, the world in which we see so little, and the parameters close in so tightly that we don't know what's really going on. Then the poet would talk about Jerusalem, which he saw as a greater world, as a reality, created through the divine imagination, which runs through all men and women.

I want to close with William Blake's ode "Jerusalem" from 1810. I hope you'll try to hear these words as Neville himself heard them.

And did those feet in ancient time
Walk upon Englands mountains green:
And was the holy Lamb of God,
On Englands pleasant pastures seen!

And did the Countenance Divine,
Shine forth upon our clouded hills?
And was Jerusalem builded here,
Among these dark Satanic Mills?

Bring me my Bow of burning gold:
Bring me my arrows of desire:
Bring me my Spear: O clouds unfold!
Bring me my Chariot of fire!

I will not cease from Mental Fight,
Nor shall my sword sleep in my hand:
Till we have built Jerusalem,
In Englands green & pleasant Land.

*   *   *

If there are a few questions, I'd be happy to take them.

Speaker: Can you do multiple wishes, say if there are three that you wish?

Mitch Horowitz: Neville's own students in his lifetime asked him that very thing, and I'm in the same place myself because it's hard sometimes to limit one's wishes to one thing. Neville felt it was more effective if you limit it to one thing at a time; but he said that this was by no means a limit, you didn't have to limit yourself. The key thing is to feel the desire intensely and to hold your mental emotive picture with clarity and simplicity, and to stick with it. He did say he felt that at the time interval would be lessened if you limit yourself to one thing at a time. That was his practice, but he did not call it a must.

Speaker: I wanted something that didn't last, so to try to achieve that, do I meditate on it? How do I get result?

MH: Neville's idea was to enact a scene that would naturally transpire when the desired thing comes to pass. There may be many events that would transpire if that thing came to pass, but he said to select just one that has a particular emotional resonance, and then see yourself doing it over and over. Something as simple as a handshake or climbing a ladder. Just take one that has act emotional gravity and be persistent.

Speaker: Do you think that given his predilection for inner vision that there's any evidence suggest that Abdullah may have been a channel? Abdullah may have been a channel or a channel within Neville?

MH: Oh, that's an interesting question. He always referred to Abdullah as a flesh-and-blood figure, and he said Abdullah lived in an apartment on West 72nd Street, which I've visited, and he would talk about Abdullah in very physical, vivid terms, so he certainly described him as a flesh-and-blood being.

Speaker: You described many of the techniques, including the technique of walking in a cold winter day to get the feeling of being in another place. This is just other technique for the astral body. Basically, what he's describing is the emotional astral body being developed, of which one expression would be manifesting that state here, but it sounds like he could easily develop another technique because this sounds very limited.

MH: He does represent techniques such as walking and imagining himself in the palm tree-lined lanes in Barbados; but he most often came back to this idea of physical immobility and the uses of a hypnagogic state, that drowsy state. He again and again said that others can experiment, and should experiment, but that he personally found that to be the simplest and the most effective method. He would say sometimes he would enter the hypnagogic state and just feel thankful or try to seize upon one expression like *it is wonderful.* He might do that if he didn't have a specific thing that he was longing for at that moment. So he did experiment with some other techniques and points of view. He did said one lecture, "You praise others and you will shine," because it was very important to try to use these techniques to the benefit of another person. For example, if you have a friend who's looking for a job, you might form the mental picture of congratulating him or her on finding the perfect job because Neville believed in the oneness of humanity in the absolute most literal sense. There was no sentimentality about it. He felt that every individual was God.

Speaker: Did he say that he believed that the universe is holographic?

MH: He would say, and again, he sometimes made statements more in passing than full on, but he would say explicitly that we live in a universe of infinite possibilities, and everything that you desire, by the very fact of desiring it, because your imagination is a creative agent, already exists. It is a question of just claiming it, which is why it's so important to think from the desire fulfilled. It doesn't matter if you open your eyes or your checkbook or anything else and, of course, reality as we presently know it comes rushing back in. You must continue to think from the wish fulfilled, which he said was tantamount to selecting a reality that already existed. Schrodinger said there's a dead/alive cat. Neville would have said there are infinite outcomes and they all exist.

Speaker: Regarding the slowness of time, I'm curious what his thoughts were as far as the timetables for his technique.

MH: He said that we experience definite time intervals and that a time interval is part of the nature of our existence. I may want a new house and I may want that house right now, and I may think from the end of having that house, but he said, in effect, "The fact of the world that we experience here and now is that the trees have to grow to produce wood. The wood has to be harvested and the carpenter has to cut it. There will be time intervals." And he would say, "Your time interval could be an hour, it could be a month, it could be weeks, it could be years." There is a time interval. You nonetheless must stick to the ideal and try to make it just exquisitely effortless. He didn't endorse using the will. This isn't about saying, "I'm going to think this way." It is going into this meditative or drowsy or hypnagogic state, picturing something that confirms the realization of your desire, and feeling it emotionally; he said that when the method fails maybe it's because you're trying too hard. Neville wanted people to understand that there is an exquisite ease that one should feel with exercises.

Speaker: It sounds like he's saying that an emphasis on pure will would upset that balance.

MH: Yes. He used the word receptivity and he used the term time interval.

Speaker: Did Neville ever include other ideas outside of his system?

MH: He made very few references to other thought systems. He would frequently quote Scripture, mostly the New Testament. He felt the New Testament was a great blueprint and metaphor for human development in the figure of Christ. He felt that the Old Testament was suggestive of the promise and the New Testament was fulfilling of the promise, and beyond that he made little reference to other thought systems. He was chiefly interested in Scripture. He would talk about numbers; he loved symbolism. In his book *Your Faith Is Your Fortune* he talked about certain aspects of the zodiac, astrology, and number symbolism; but as time passed, he made fewer references to other systems. Every now and again he'd use a piece of language where I'll detect Emile Coué echoed; but so much of what we talked about really came from his own description of the world through his own experience. He made little reference to other systems.

Speaker: I started reading your book *Occult America* and there was a question in my mind—you write that a lot of positive thinkers and people in New Age in American history have, on the one hand, kind of advocated basic techniques and methods for selfish success and money, and, on the other hand, a lot of the better writers in New Age and New Thought were passionately involved with and concerned about social movements. Where did Neville fall in that dichotomy?

MH: That's a wonderful question and that was an aspect for me that made it difficult to first enter Neville's work, because he had no social concerns in the conventional sense, and if people raised social concerns, he would push them aside and would insist that the world you see, whether it is of beauty or violence, is self-created. Prove the theory to yourself and then use the theory as you wish. You want to eliminate suffering? Eliminate suffering. But he ardently rejected fealty to any kind of social movement or ideal. He believed that coming into one's awareness of the godlike nature of imagination, of the literal God presence of the imagination, of having the experience of being reborn through one's skull, was the essential human task.

Speaker: As you said in your own book, a lot the 19th century Spiritualists were involved in movements like suffragism and abolitionism.

MH: Yes. Well, you know, these radical movements, radical political movements and radical spiritual movements, avant-garde politics, avant-garde spirituality, they all intersect. We often fail to understand how a figure like Marcus Garvey, for example, was involved with mental metaphysics; but as you get closer to the real lives of these people, the connection becomes more natural because they craved a new social order both spiritually and socially.

Ideals Realized:

Aphorisms by Neville

"Believing and being are one."   —radio lecture, 1951

"If we would become as emotionally aroused over our ideals as we become over our dislikes, we would ascend to the plane of our ideals as easily as we now descend to the level of our hates."

—The Search, 1946

"Imagination travels according to habit."

—Awakened Imagination, 1954

"We become the embodiment of that which we mentally feed upon."   *—Five Lessons*, 1948

"Today's events are bound to disturb yesterday's established order. Imaginative men and women invariably unsettle a preexisting peace of mind."

—side one, "The Secret of Imagining," vinyl album, 1960

"An assumption will harden into fact, if persisted in."

—quoted in *The Los Angeles Times*, July 7, 1951

"The acceptance of the end—the acceptance of the answered prayer—finds the means for its realization."

—radio lecture, July 1953

"Don't blame; only resolve."

—*Awakened Imagination*, 1954

"All things are possible to the inner man."

—television talk, 1955

"For this whole wonderful world around us is nothing more than the appeasement of hunger; that's why we built it. We made it to satisfy our longing."

—television talk, 1955

"Dare to assume you are exactly *what* you want to be. Dare to assume you are *where* you want to be even though your reason and your senses deny it. If you do, will it work? It doesn't cost you a penny to try it. You are told, 'Come buy wine, buy milk without money.' Try it. Try to prove me wrong."

—undated lecture, *Immortal Man*, 1977

"Duty has no momentum."

—*Awakened Imagination*, 1954

"A man's mental conversations attracts his life."

—lecture, 1955

"There would be no progress in the world were it not for the divine discontent in man which urges him on to higher and higher levels of consciousness."

—radio lecture, 1951

"Then I'll tell it to the bare walls"

—Neville circa late 1960s to a speaking agent warned him to stop emphasizing esoteric material in his talks or he would lose his audience. (See *The Miracle Club*)

"Nothing stands between man and the fulfillment of his dream but facts, and facts are the creations of imagining."

—side one, "The Secret of Imagining," vinyl album, 1960

"Do not try to change people; they are only messengers telling you who you are. Revalue yourself and they will confirm the change."

　　　　　　　—*Your Faith is Your Fortune*, 1941

"Fools exploit the world; the wise transfigure it."

　　　　　　　—*Prayer: The Art of Believing*, 1945

Prophet In His Own Country:

A Neville Goddard Timeline

1905—Neville Lancelot Goddard is born on February 19 to a British family in St. Michael, Barbados, the fourth child in a family of nine boys and one girl.

1922—At age seventeen Neville relocates to New York City to study theater. He makes a career as an actor and dancer on stage and silent screen, landing roles on Broadway, silent film, and touring Europe as part of a dance troupe.

1923—Neville briefly marries Mildred Mary Hughes, with whom he has a son, Joseph Goddard, born the following year.

1929—Neville marked this as the year that begin his mystical journey: "Early in the morning, maybe about three-thirty or four o'clock, I was taken in spirit into the Divine Council where the gods hold converse." (lecture from *Immortal Man*, 1977)

1931—After several years of occult study, Neville meets his teacher Abdullah, a turbaned black man of Jewish descent. The pair work together for five years in New York City.

1938—Neville begins his own teaching and speaking.

1939—Neville's first book, *At Your Command*, is published.

1940-1941—Neville meets Catherine Willa Van Schumus, who is to become his second wife.

1941—Neville publishes his longer and more ambitious book, *Your Faith Is Your Fortune*.

1942—Neville marries Catherine, who later that year gives birth to their daughter Victoria. Also that year, Neville publishes *Freedom for All: A Practical Application of the Bible*.

1942-1943—From November to March, Neville serves in the military before returning home to Greenwich Village in New York City. In 1943, Neville is profiled in *The New Yorker.*

1944—Neville publishes *Feeling Is the Secret.*

1945—Neville publishes *Prayer: The Art of Believing.*

1946—Neville meets mystical philosopher Israel Regardie in New York, who profiles him in his book *The Romance of Metaphysics.* Neville also publishes his pamphlet *The Search.*

1948—Neville delivers his classic "Five Lessons" lectures in Los Angeles, which many students find the clearest and most compelling summation of his methodology. It appears posthumously as a book.

1949—Neville publishes *Out of This World: Thinking Fourth Dimensionally.*

1952—Neville publishes *The Power of Awareness.*

1954—Neville publishes *Awakened Imagination.*

1955—Neville hosts radio and television shows in Los Angeles.

1956—Neville publishes *Seedtime and Harvest: A Mystical View of the Scriptures.*

1959—Neville undergoes the mystical experience of being reborn from his own skull. Other mystical experiences follow into the following year.

1960—Neville releases a spoken-word album.

1961—Neville publishes *The Law and Promise*; the final chapter, "The Promise," details the mystical experience he underwent in 1959, and others that followed.

1964—Neville publishes the pamphlet *He Breaks the Shell: A Lesson in Scripture.*

1966—Neville publishes his last full-length book, *Resurrection*, composed of four works from the 1940s and the contemporaneous closing title essay, which outlines the fullness of his mystical vision and of humanity's realization of its deific nature.

1972—Neville dies in West Hollywood at age 67 on October 1, 1972 from an "apparent heart attack" reports the *Los Angeles Times*. He is buried at the family plot in St. Michael, Barbados.

ABOUT THE AUTHORS

Neville Goddard was one of the most remarkable mystical thinkers of the past century. In more than ten books and thousands of lectures, Neville, under his solitary first name, expanded on one core principle: *the human imagination is God.* As such, he taught, everything that you experience results from your thoughts and feeling states. Born to an Anglican family in Barbados in 1905, Neville traveled to New York City at age seventeen in 1922 to study theater. Although he won roles on Broadway, in silent films, and toured internationally with a dance troupe, Neville abandoned acting in the early 1930s to dedicate himself to metaphysical studies and embark a new career as a writer and lecturer. He was a compelling presence at metaphysical churches, spiritual centers, and auditoriums until his death in West Hollywood, California, in 1972. Neville was not widely known during his lifetime, but today his books and lectures have attained new popularity. Neville's principles about the creative properties of the mind prefigured some of today's most radical quantum theorizing, and have influenced several major spiritual writers, including Carlos Castaneda and Joseph Murphy.

Mitch Horowitz is a PEN Award-winning historian whose books include *Occult America*, *One Simple Idea*, *The Miracle Club*, and *The Miracle Habits*. His book *Awakened Mind* is one of the first works of New Thought translated and published in Arabic. The Chinese government has censored his work. Twitter @MitchHorowitz | Instagram @MitchHorowitz23